Quest
for the
Lost City
of
Gold

by
STEPHEN BIESTY

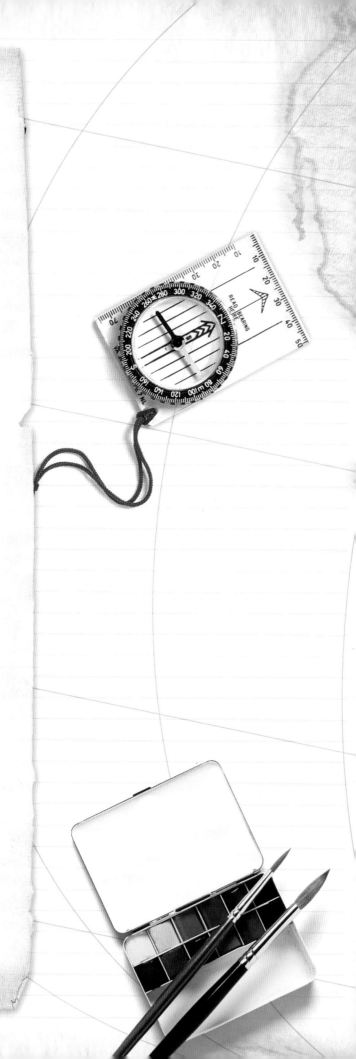

DK

LONDON, NEW YORK,
MELBOURNE, MUNICH, AND DELHI

Written by Samone Bos

Inside-out illustrations by Stephen Biesty

Editor Jenny Finch
Designers Spencer Holbrook, Hoa Luc
Senior Editor Julie Ferris
Senior Art Editor Stefan Podhorodecki

Managing Editor Linda Esposito
Managing Art Editor Diane Thistlethwaite
Design Development Manager Sophia M Tampakopolous Turner
Publishing Manager Andrew Macintyre
Category Publisher Laura Buller
Picture Researchers Jenny Baskaya
DK Picture Library Claire Bowers
Production Controller Georgina Hayworth
DTP Designer Siu Chan
Jacket Editor Mariza O'Keeffe
Jacket Designer Stefan Podhorodecki

Editorial Consultant Philip Wilkinson

Buildings Consultants Professor Sir John Boardman,
Dr Brian O'Callaghan, Dr Anne Millard, David Murdoch,
Philip Parker, Dr Peter Sharrock, Philip Wilkinson

First published in Great Britain in 2007 by
Dorling Kindersley Limited,
80 Strand, London WC2R 0RL

2 4 6 8 10 9 7 5 3 1
BD327 – 08/07

ISBN: 978-1-40532-187-7
Printed and bound by Hung Hing, China

Discover more at
www.dk.com

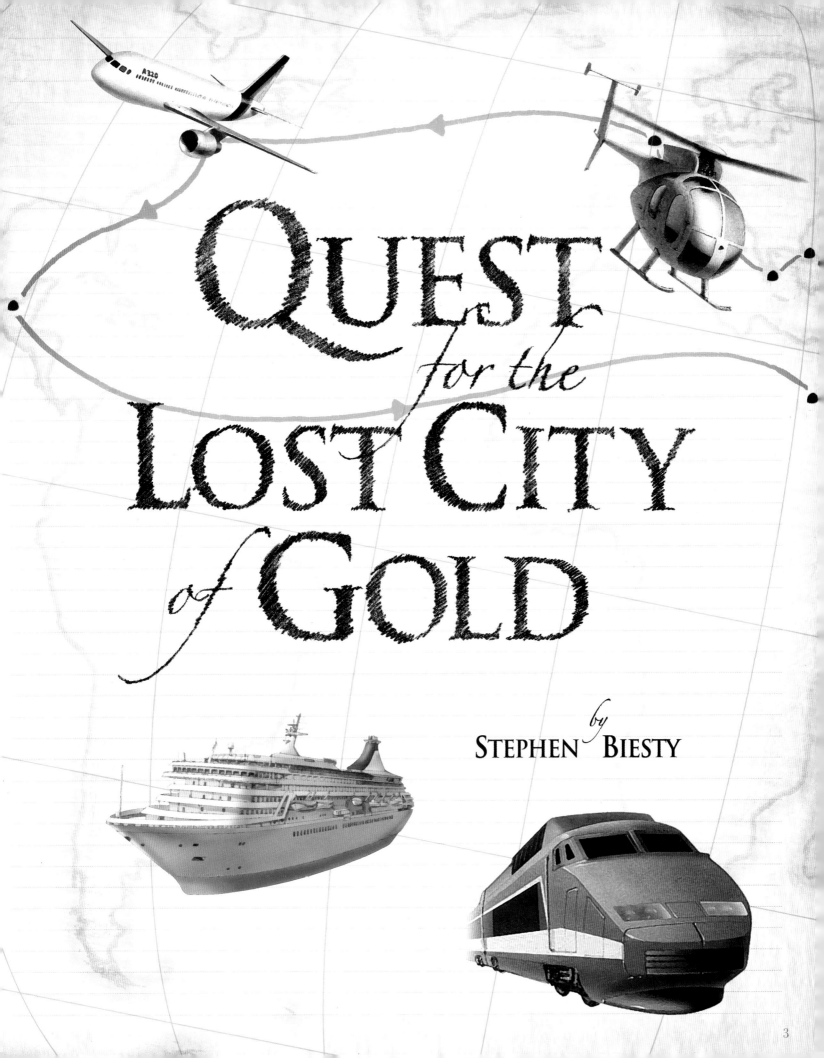

QUEST
for the
LOST CITY
of GOLD

by
STEPHEN BIESTY

The quest begins

This is the letter from Jack that started the whole quest.

Dear Steve,

It's your old history teacher, Jack Smith. Remember me? Nowadays, I have retired from teaching, and have been travelling the world. I have found out about many cultures, sampled their food, and seen so many great buildings, museums, and landscapes. I truly feel like I've seen the world inside and out.

I hope you have some time on your hands, because I am inviting you on a quest to find an ancient lost city. It involves two of my favourite topics — history and architecture. Don't worry — I'm covering all the costs!

Next week, I'll send you a postcard asking you to visit a famous building somewhere in the world. I'm not going to make it too easy — the postcard will simply give you clues to the building's whereabouts. Once you are there, I'd like you to draw the building as it was at a significant time in its history. Then you'll receive another postcard sending you to the next location.

Sound tough? Well, I think you're up to the challenge!

However, there's a slight catch. I know you are good at drawing, and always got top marks in history, but I hope you are good with numbers, too. In each postcard, I will give you a riddle. The answer to this riddle is always going to be a number related to the place you're visiting. Maybe it will be something you can count, or you might have to do a little more research to find the answer.

To make it a little easier, I've already given you the answers on a card. Simply mark off each number as you solve each riddle. At the end of your quest, you will be left with just two numbers.

Why?

Well, Steve, that's a surprise I'm keeping for later...

Look out for the first postcard!

Yours intrepidly,

Jack Smith

Something tells me I might be off on a journey very soon...

RIDDLE CARD

COVER THE ANSWER TO EACH RIDDLE WITH A STICKER. TWO NUMBERS SHOULD REMAIN.

40	17	1,000
28	617	3
134	4	73
70	10,154	8

N
W · E
S

When I was at school, I had a history teacher named Jack Smith. He would tell my class so many great stories — everything from the ancient Incas right through to the world wars and first humans in space.

One year ago, I received a letter from Jack, inviting me on a quest. This quest took me all over the world, and I recorded my travels in this journal. Jack asked me to visit buildings of the world, and draw them at an important time in history. I decided to take things a step further and draw them "inside and out". You'll soon see what I mean...

Jack led me to each destination with a simple postcard. But the postcard wasn't really THAT simple! I had to follow clues to identify the location, and solve riddles to collect numbers along the way. Is your brain hurting already? The surprise at the end made all this number-crunching worth it!

You might not be able to hop on the next plane, but you can use this journal to relive my adventures and set off on a quest of your own.

The riddle card is in a pocket at the back of this journal. Take it out and, as you solve the riddles, cross off the numbers on the card or cover them with the sticker stamps.

I think I'd better pack my bags! Mustn't forget my sketching kit...

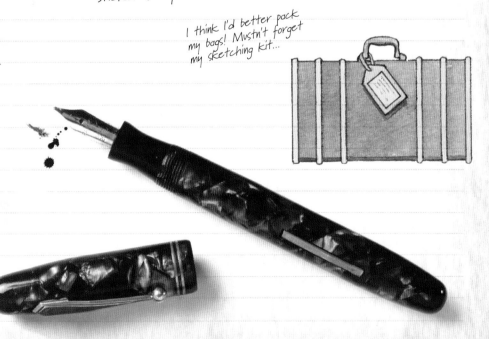

Dear Diary...

Setting off on the quest tomorrow morning. First stop Sydney. I wonder what awaits me there?

Sydney Opera House

The Sydney Opera House overlooks Australia's Sydney Harbour. Resembling a flotilla of sailboats, its unique billowing structure has made it an icon of 20th-century design. A popular tourist attraction, the Opera House is home to various performing arts, from opera and theatre, to ballet and contemporary dance.

G'DAY STEVE,

OVER THE ROARING SURF I CAN HEAR AN ITALIAN ARIA, BUT I'M A LONG WAY FROM EUROPE. THESE SHELLS HOUSE MORE THAN OPERA THOUGH. WHAT ELSE SHOULD THIS POSTCARD HARBOUR? THAT'S RIGHT — A RIDDLE!

THE PLUMBING IS WRONG —
NO, IT ISN'T A SEWER,
YOU'LL COUNT THOUSANDS OF THESE,
AND NOT ANY FEWER.

Jack

STEPHEN BIESTY
BONSAI MANOR,
SOMERSET,
UK

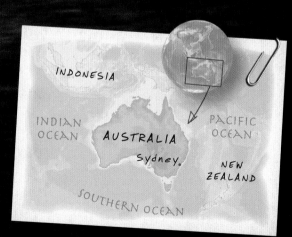

INDONESIA

INDIAN OCEAN

AUSTRALIA
Sydney.

PACIFIC OCEAN

NEW ZEALAND

SOUTHERN OCEAN

In January 1958, the first Opera House Lottery was drawn to fund construction of the massive project. Over 16 years, 496 lotteries raised 101 million Australian dollars to pay for the Opera House, though it was originally estimated to cost just $7 million.

It took me 27 hours and two planes to get here, but it seems I've finally started the quest. When Jack greeted me with "G'day!", I knew he was in Australia.

When I read "Italian aria", the first thing that came to mind was the opera. And where would you find the opera in Australia? The Sydney Opera House, of course!

So, Jack wants me to draw the Opera House. I'm looking around for something to count, but where should I start? I think I'd better take a closer look at that riddle.

The Opera House backs onto parkland on Bennelong Point. The structure is 183 m (600 ft) long and 120 m (393 ft) wide.

The Sydney Opera House is an international symbol of Australia. It featured in the 2000 Sydney Olympics logo as an instantly recognizable "squiggle".

THE ARCHITECT
Danish architect Jørn Utzon won a competition to design the Sydney Opera House, beating 233 entries. Utzon fell out with the financiers and resigned before construction was completed. He never saw the finished building.

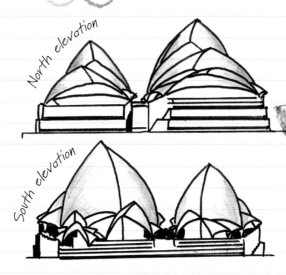

North elevation

South elevation

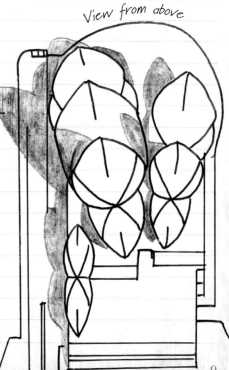

View from above

The Opera House has ten sail-like "shells," housing five different theatres, shops, and a restaurant. It took 14 years to build, with the interior finally completed in 1973.

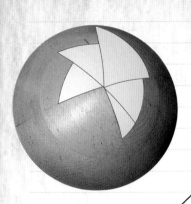

SPHERICAL SOLUTION

In 1961, the engineers who were working on the building realized that the Opera House roofs could be designed as though they were all sliced off the same sphere. This was one of the first times computers were used in structural design.

UNDER CONSTRUCTION

Large sections of the Opera House were assembled on site and winched into place with three tower cranes. Inside, 2,400 concrete ribs support the structure.

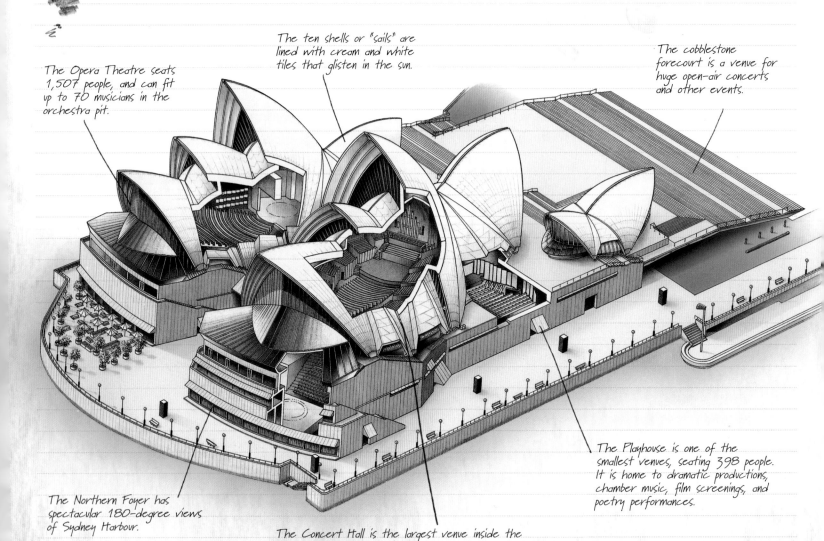

The Opera Theatre seats 1,507 people, and can fit up to 70 musicians in the orchestra pit.

The ten shells or "sails" are lined with cream and white tiles that glisten in the sun.

The cobblestone forecourt is a venue for huge open-air concerts and other events.

The Northern Foyer has spectacular 180-degree views of Sydney Harbour.

The Concert Hall is the largest venue inside the Opera House, seating 2,679 people.

The Playhouse is one of the smallest venues, seating 398 people. It is home to dramatic productions, chamber music, film screenings, and poetry performances.

OPEN-AIR EVENTS

The forecourt is a popular venue for concerts and city celebrations, such as the spectacular fireworks displays that mark the New Year.

PILES OF TILES

The roofs are covered with 1,056,056 glazed granite tiles, imported from Sweden. Laid in a chevron (v-shaped) pattern, the tiles self-clean when it rains. Specialist staff must abseil around the steep curves of the building to perform maintenance checks and repairs.

AWESOME ORGAN

Completed in 1979, the Concert Hall's Grand Organ is the world's largest mechanical organ. With 10,154 pipes, it took 10 years to build.

I got tickets for a concert while visiting and it has inspired me to draw the Concert Hall of the Opera House during a classical concert. Things are slowly starting to add up...

Speaking of "adding up", I've had a look at that riddle for something to count. "Plumbing" is an odd word to associate with an Opera House — maybe I need to look for pipes of a different kind?

TIMELINE

1788
Governor Arthur Phillip names Bennelong Point after an Aboriginal man he befriends there.

1947
Eugene Goossens, conductor of the Sydney Symphony, proposes an opera theatre is built on Bennelong Point.

1957
Danish architect Jørn Utzon wins a government competition to design the Sydney Opera House.

Utzon, J

1959
Construction begins on the foundations.

1963
Construction begins on the roof vaults.

1966
Jørn Utzon resigns from his position in a storm of controversy.

1967
Architects Hall, Todd, and Littlemore design the interior.

20 October, 1973
Queen Elizabeth II officially opens the Opera House.

Today
More than 250,000 people attend the Opera House's guided tours each year.

11

Inside the Opera House

1. The 10 tiled "shells" are in fact concrete panels supported by an inner skeleton of concrete ribs.

2. A mixture of matt and shiny chevron-shaped glazed tiles are arranged in a pattern that reflects the light.

3. The 25-m- (82-ft-) high ceiling is fitted with 18 acoustic rings, which partly deflect the sound of instruments back to the stage to help the musicians to hear their performance.

4. Sydney Symphony Orchestra is performing a Beethoven symphony.

5. The Grand Organ – the world's largest pipe organ – took 10 years to build.

6. Awash with ships and leisure boats, Sydney Harbour forms an impressive backdrop for the Opera House, which is surrounded by water on three sides.

7. Glass panels fill the open ends of the shells.

8. The Concert Hall is the largest auditorium in the complex, seating 2,679 people. The seats are upholstered in purple wool.

9. There are about 1,000 rooms in the Opera House, as well as the performance venues, including rehearsal rooms and a restaurant.

10. The interior walls are covered in white birch plywood and Australian brush-box wood.

SOUTHEAST
ASIA

Siem Reap · CAMBODIA

GULF
OF
THAILAND

SOUTH CHINA SEA

le
st

ds.

ANGKOR WAT

In the dense jungle outskirts of Siem Reap, Cambodia, Angkor Wat ("city temple") is a sprawling temple famous for its elaborate stone carvings. It was built between 1113 and 1150 for King Suryavarman II, who ruled over the vast Khmer Empire. Hundreds of visitors gather behind the lily-flecked pond before dawn to witness the ancient temple "appear" as the sun rises between its lotus-shaped towers.

Dear Steve,

The deepest jungle is where I have anchored, so to speak. No, I don't have a boat — but there is a moat. Before me looms the crown of the Khmer Empire, once Hindu, now Buddhist. Confused? Don't worry — you will soon work out what's wat!

Statues line this hall of fame. Do not count, just read the name.

Jack

2.25

Stephen Biesty
c/o Goanna
Guesthouse,
Sydney,
Australia

CAMBODIA: Siem Reap, Temple

Jack certainly was being tricky here, saying that he was anchored without a boat. I found it helpful to read the postcard aloud a few times... eventually Angkor rolled off my tongue!

I realized I was on the right track when I saw that Jack forgot the "h" in "what". I knew this had to be on purpose. Jack's eagle eye would never miss a spelling error. So "wat" it was!

Jack is right — Angkor Wat was the crown of the Khmer Empire. I once read about the many lavish celebrations King Suryavarman II held here, including a grand parade for his 30th birthday in 1130.

CHANGING RELIGION

Originally dedicated to the Hindu god Vishnu, Angkor Wat became a Buddhist shrine in the 1300s. Beside the main entrance stands a stone statue that previously represented Vishnu. When Angkor Wat became Buddhist, the statue of Vishnu was worshipped as a special Buddha for the Angkor area, but a reminder of the statue's former identity is its eight hands, each carrying symbols of Vishnu.

Angkor Wat has featured on every version of the Cambodian national flag since the country's first flag in 1863.

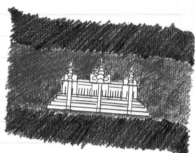

Khmer Empire shaded red

Today's Cambodia

THE KHMER EMPIRE

When Angkor Wat was built, the Khmer Empire (802–1434) was at its height. This map shows the empire's extent c.1150, when it covered modern-day Cambodia, Laos, and most of Thailand and Vietnam.

THE MOAT

Measuring 200 m (656 ft) wide and 3.6 km (2.2 miles) long, Angkor Wat's moat helped keep the jungle at bay over the many years the temple was neglected.

These lads from a local village are in the moat collecting water plants in a woven basket.

15

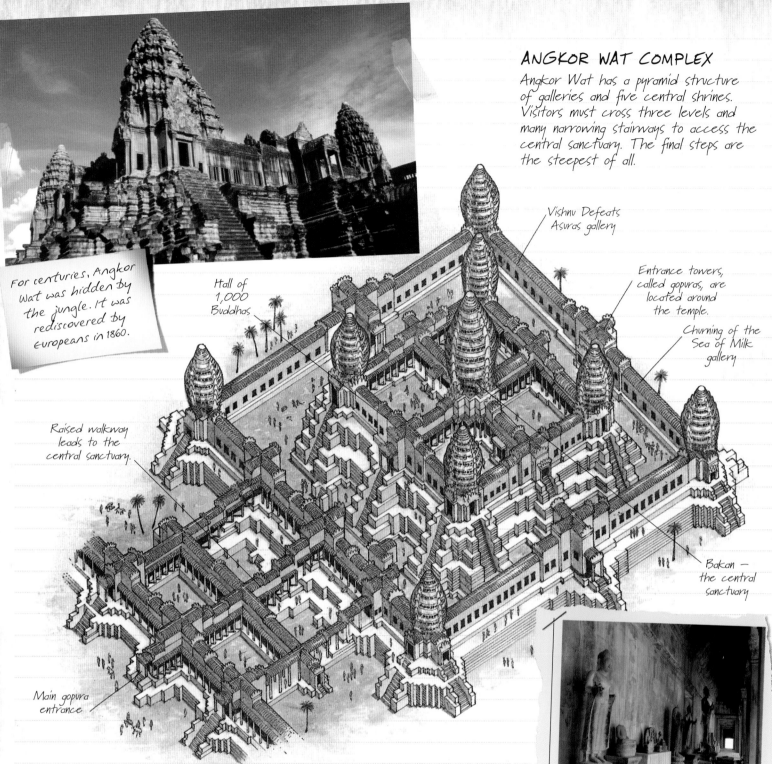

ANGKOR WAT COMPLEX
Angkor Wat has a pyramid structure of galleries and five central shrines. Visitors must cross three levels and many narrowing stairways to access the central sanctuary. The final steps are the steepest of all.

For centuries, Angkor Wat was hidden by the jungle. It was rediscovered by Europeans in 1860.

Vishnu Defeats Asuras gallery

Entrance towers, called gopuras, are located around the temple.

Churning of the Sea of Milk gallery

Hall of 1,000 Buddhas

Raised walkway leads to the central sanctuary.

Bakan — the central sanctuary

Main gopura entrance

STONE CARVINGS
Angkor Wat's long galleries are covered in carvings. The Churning of the Sea of Milk gallery includes carvings of a giant naga (serpent or dragon), marine creatures, 92 asuras (demons), and 88 devas (gods). The carvings in the photograph are apsarases (beautiful nymphs).

HALL OF 1,000 BUDDHAS
Bridging the outer gallery to the second enclosure, the walls of this hall are lined with many statues of Buddha, which are inscribed in Khmer, Burmese, and Japanese characters. The four courtyards beside the hall contained pools of sacred water.

CAMBODIA: Angkor Wat,

QUIET PLEASE!

Angkor Wat's entrance is flanked by two "libraries", but there are no books in these buildings, despite the name. They are smaller temples, or shrines.

I am a little bleary-eyed today after getting up so early to see the sun rise — but it was worth it. Now I really must tackle this riddle. I wonder which hall of fame Jack is talking about? In the march to the central sanctuary, Angkor Wat feels like a maze of halls!

So, I should be keeping a keen eye out for statues. Strangely, while I go searching for my figure, Jack is telling me "Do not count, just read the name!" Maybe this will be easier than I thought...

This picture shows Ta Phrom, a neighbouring temple in Angkor where trees and wandering vines strangle the structure. It reminds me of an old horror movie!

LAST LEG

Known as the bakan, the central sanctuary is accessed via three sets of very steep stairways. Skirted by four corner towers, a central tower shoots 43 m (141 ft) into the sky. Together, the five towers represent the five peaks of Mount Meru, home of the Hindu gods. The steep steps are said to symbolize the long and hazardous journey to the heavens.

TIMELINE

1100–1175
Angkor Wat is built.

1369
Thais attack the city of Angkor and briefly take control.

1600s
A Japanese pilgrim draws Angkor. He thinks it is in India.

1860
French colonize Cambodia and discover the Angkor ruins.

1992
Angkor Wat is included on UNESCO World Heritage List.

1432
Khmer Empire falls. Buddhist monks move into Angkor.

1500s
Khmers return and establish Angkor Wat as a Buddhist shrine.

1600s
Portuguese dub Angkor "the walled city".

1960s
Restoration work commences on Angkor Wat.

1970s–1980s
Civil war stops restoration.

Inside Angkor Wat

1. The moat encircling the temple stretches 3.6 km (2.2 miles).

2. Stone statue of Vishnu stands beneath the southern tower.

3. Outer enclosure contains ponds, libraries, and a small village of dwellings.

4. Causeway across the moat leads to the outer wall of the temple. In the wall's corner pavilions are the "Elephant Gates" — named after their size and ability to admit the massive creatures in processions and festivities.

5. The five towers represent the peaks of Mount Meru (home of the gods according to Hindu beliefs).

6. Steep and slippery steps lead to the central sanctuary. These levels were only for the Brahmins (priests) who connected earthly beings with the divine gods.

7. Parade in celebration of king Suryavarman II's 30th birthday. He leads the Brahmins into the new state temple to get Vishnu's blessing for his armies, who are about to go into battle.

8. Central courtyard is on the temple's highest level and only the king and the most important priests are allowed access.

9. Over decades, teams of slaves and master craftsmen pieced together the sandstone blocks that make up the temple.

10. Intricate carvings and sculptures adorn every part of the complex.

its

an

le

Hagia Sophia

HAGIA SOPHIA

Built between 532 and 537 CE, Hagia Sophia was the main Christian church of Constantinople (now Istanbul in Turkey), the capital of the Byzantine Empire. In 1453 the empire fell to the Ottomans, and the church was converted into a Muslim mosque. It is regarded as one of the finest structures of the Byzantine era.

In 1935, Hagia Sophia had its most recent conversion when it became a museum.

EUROPE

BLACK SEA

Istanbul
TURKEY

MEDITERRANEAN SEA

ASIA

DEAR STEVE,

IT IS DOUBLE THE FUN IN THESE PARTS! WITH EUROPE EAST AND ASIA WEST, THIS CITY SPANS TWO CONTINENTS. HERE, YOU WILL FIND MANY EXQUISITE MOSQUES AND CHURCHES — BUT THE MUSEUM I'M LOOKING AT HAS BEEN BOTH IN ITS TIME. PUZZLED? PERHAPS THIS RIDDLE WILL HELP YOU SEE CLEARLY...

A HALF-ORB GLOWS, PIERCED WITH LIGHT, HOW MANY "EYES" ARE WITHOUT SIGHT?

Jack

STEPHEN BIESTY
c/o ANGKOR INN,
SIEM REAP,
CAMBODIA

JUSTINIAN'S JOY

Justinian I was the Byzantine emperor who presided over the construction of Hagia Sophia. Two other churches had previously been built on the site, but Justinian's was so lavish he is said to have exclaimed: "Solomon, I have surpassed thee!" (Solomon was a great king in the Bible who built many fine palaces and the Temple in Jerusalem.)

In Greek, "Hagia" means divine, and "Sophia" means wisdom. In Turkish, the building is known as "Ayasofya".

BYZANTINE EMPIRE

The Roman Empire was divided in the 300s CE, and the eastern part became known as the Byzantine Empire. The Byzantines were Greek-speaking Christians.

Jack's right — it is double the fun around here! Istanbul is famous for bridging Europe and Asia, so that clue was quite easy. There is so much fascinating history in this place.

When Jack mentioned it had once been a church, a mosque, and now a museum, I realized he had to be talking about Hagia Sophia, so here I am. It is certainly an impressive building — surrounded by minarets (mosque towers), the great dome looming in the sky looks amazing.

So, on to the clue — I'm looking for "eyes" without sight. Better get a move on...

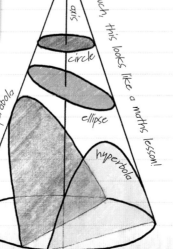

Byzantine crosses have crossbars near their bases.

CONIC SECTIONS

Isidore of Miletus, a physics teacher, and Anthemius of Tralles, a professor of geometry, were the architects behind Hagia Sophia. Anthemius's theories on conic sections helped mastermind Hagia Sophia's complicated vaults (arched ceilings).

Ouch, this looks like a maths lesson!

axis

circle

parabola

ellipse

hyperbola

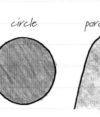

circle	parabola	ellipse	hyperbola

When you cut a cone at right angles to its axis, a circle is formed.

When you cut the cone parallel to the side of the cone, a parabola is formed.

Between the circle and the parabola is an ellipse (elongated circle).

When you cut the cone parallel to its axis, a hyperbola is formed.

RICH HERITAGE

When the Muslim Ottomans conquered Istanbul in 1453, Hagia Sophia was converted into a mosque. The ruler Mehmed II plastered over the Christian mosaics and frescoes. Over time, four minarets were added. Change came again in 1935 when the building was transformed into a museum. Since then, care has been taken to balance the building's Muslim and Christian heritages.

THE DOME

The huge dome is lined with 40 arched windows, which flood the building with light. In 558, the original dome was destroyed by an earthquake and had to be rebuilt.

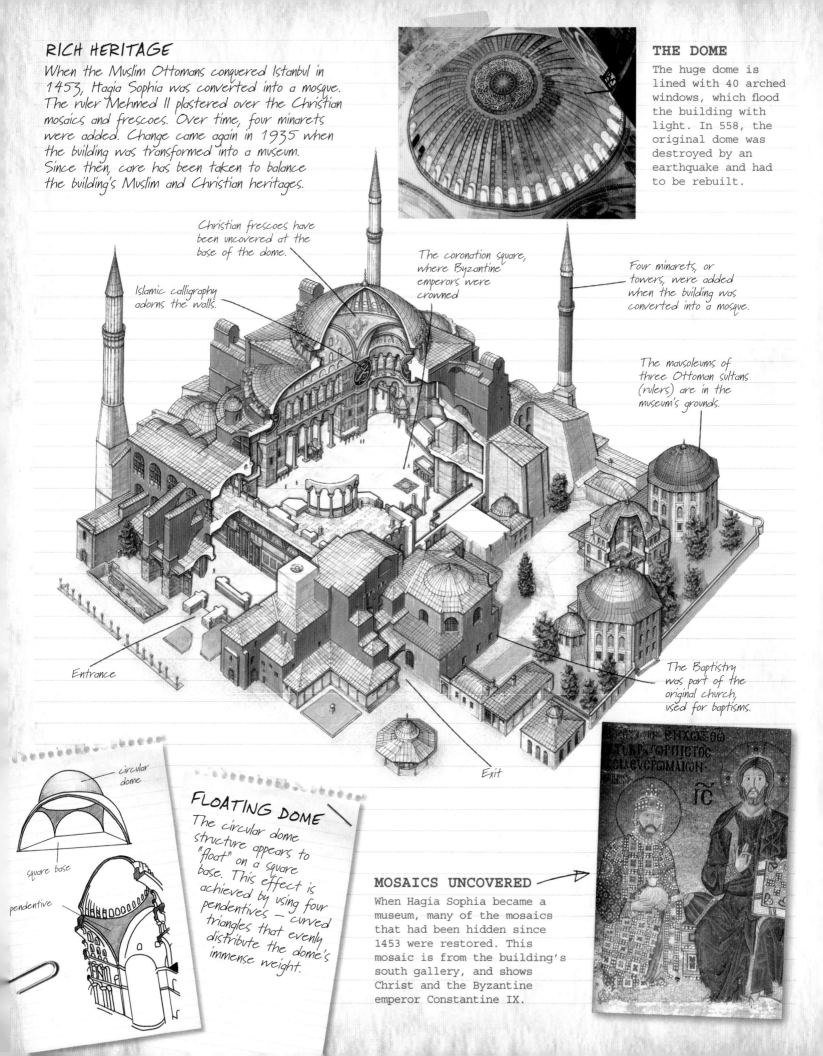

Christian frescoes have been uncovered at the base of the dome.

Islamic calligraphy adorns the walls.

The coronation square, where Byzantine emperors were crowned

Four minarets, or towers, were added when the building was converted into a mosque.

The mausoleums of three Ottoman sultans (rulers) are in the museum's grounds.

Entrance

The Baptistry was part of the original church, used for baptisms.

Exit

FLOATING DOME

The circular dome structure appears to "float" on a square base. This effect is achieved by using four pendentives — curved triangles that evenly distribute the dome's immense weight.

circular dome

square base

pendentive

MOSAICS UNCOVERED

When Hagia Sophia became a museum, many of the mosaics that had been hidden since 1453 were restored. This mosaic is from the building's south gallery, and shows Christ and the Byzantine emperor Constantine IX.

LAVISH INTERIOR

While the exterior had plain walls, inside Hagia Sophia the Byzantines cloaked every surface with exquisite marble panels and glittering gold mosaics. The roundels (round boards with Islamic calligraphy) were added when the building became a mosque.

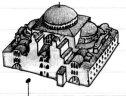

AN INSPIRATION

Hagia Sophia inspired the design of many mosques during the Ottoman rule of Istanbul. The Blue Mosque (left), built in the 1600s opposite Hagia Sophia, was meant to rival its neighbour in size and splendour.

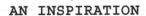

Scattered outside Hagia Sophia are 550-year-old cannonballs that were used in the battle for Constantinople in 1453.

"Perhaps this riddle will help you see clearly." Jack must be joking! I get the feeling I'll never see straight with all these riddles to solve.

Jack clearly doesn't mean real eyes, so I'm looking for something that's "pierced with light". I think I've solved the first part of the clue though — "a half orb" can only mean one thing here. An orb is a ball shape, so half an orb must mean the dome.

There's so much history to this place that it was hard to decide what to draw, but I've decided to go for its first incarnation — as a Christian church.

TIMELINE

360
Constantinople's founder, Emperor Constantine, dedicates Megale Ekklesia (Great Church) on site of Hagia Sophia.

404
Church is destroyed in riots. In 415 a second church is built on the same site by Emperor Theodosius II.

532
A revolt in the city destroys church.

537
Hagia Sophia completed and consecrated as a Christian church by Emperor Justinian I.

558
Dome collapses in earthquake, requiring a rebuild.

562
Dome collapses again, requiring another rebuild.

1453
Ottomans conquer Constantinople and rename it Istanbul. They convert Hagia Sophia into a mosque.

1935
Turkish leader Mustafa Kemal Atatürk orders conversion of Hagia Sophia into a museum. The plaster is gradually removed from the frescoes and mosaics.

1985
Site added to UNESCO World Heritage List.

Inside Hagia Sophia

1. During Christian times, Hagia Sophia's colossal dome was richly decorated with figures of saints.

2. The ambo (pulpit) is placed in silver and gold, and studded with gemstones and ivory carvings.

3. The chancel screen separates the altar from the nave (central space).

4. Emperor Justinian and his wife Theodora lead a long procession of priests and attendants in a ceremony to establish Hagia Sophia as the religious centre of the Byzantine Empire.

5. Fortified city walls span 6,492 m (22,300 ft) and beyond them lies the Bosphorus, a narrow strait of water.

6. Forty windows around the base of the great dome fill the nave with light, revealing surfaces panelled with glittering mosaics.

7. There are 107 purple and green marble columns on the ground floor and galleries (balconies).

8. Curved pendentives allow the dome to seemingly float above the square base, distributing its weight evenly across the structure.

9. An assortment of clergy and soldiers stand in the nave, watching the ceremony unfold.

10. The original walls could not bear the weight of the dome and slowly buckled outwards, before finally collapsing in 558.

The Parthenon

When I climbed up the rocky hill and snapped this photo I thought: Wow, it's HUGE!

THE PARTHENON

Looming on the Acropolis, a hill in the centre of Athens, the Parthenon is a symbol of Ancient Greece. The marble temple was built between 447–432 BCE to house a giant statue of Athena, the city's patron goddess. The temple was decorated with carvings showing tales from Greek mythology, including Athena's birth from the head of her father Zeus, and her battle with the god Poseidon (see above).

GREECE: Athens, Temple

Dear Steve,

I stopped by to visit a Greek goddess, but she's left her home in RUINS! Long ago, her birthday parties were huge. And what an excuse to dress up! Now, I've thought long and hard about this riddle, Steve. I looked up, down, and all around...

Tall like soldiers of marbled rank, serving patiently on the left flank.

I hope you're still keeping count.

Jack

Stephen Biesty
Room 1500,
Ottoman Hotel,
Istanbul,
TURKEY

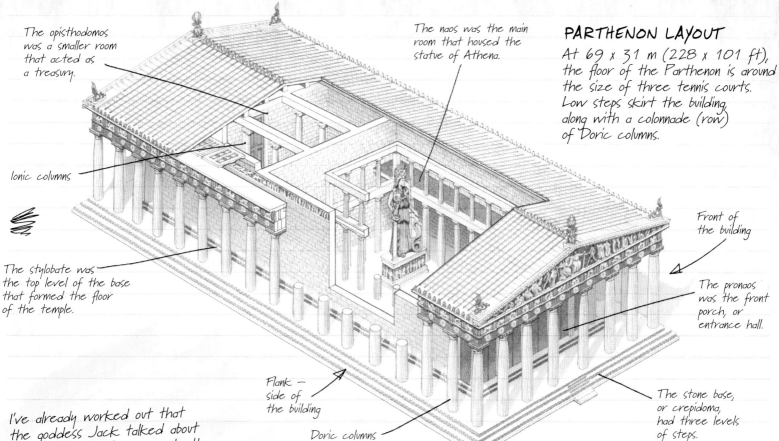

PARTHENON LAYOUT

At 69 x 31 m (228 x 101 ft), the floor of the Parthenon is around the size of three tennis courts. Low steps skirt the building, along with a colonnade (row) of Doric columns.

The opisthodomos was a smaller room that acted as a treasury.

The naos was the main room that housed the statue of Athena.

Ionic columns

Front of the building

The stylobate was the top level of the base that formed the floor of the temple.

The pronaos was the front porch, or entrance hall.

Flank — side of the building

Doric columns

The stone base, or crepidoma, had three levels of steps.

I've already worked out that the goddess Jack talked about was Athena, so I've come to the Parthenon — her most famous temple. I wonder when her birthday was? Did people dress up to celebrate?

Soldiers and flank strike me as important words in the riddle. Could this mean REAL soldiers or something trickier? Flank is a military word, but does it also mean a part of a building?

While I'm puzzling over this, I can't help but think of all the great minds that met here. Sophocles, Aristotle, Euripides, Plato... I'm getting a serious headache!

Time is ticking away... I just HOPE I'm doing my sums right.

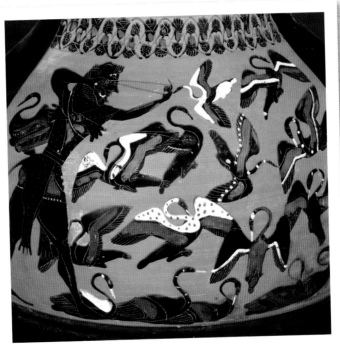

Wool or linen robes were coloured with plant dyes.

PLATO

Plato (427–347 BCE) was a great Athenian philosopher. He theorized about a new type of government called the Republic, where citizens could elect officials called "guardians". Scholars still study his writings to this day.

Plato

THE GOLDEN AGE

The Parthenon was built during the period known as Athens' Golden Age (480–430 BCE), when arts, literature, and philosophy flourished in the city. Art often depicted stories from Greek mythology. This vase shows the story of the hero Herakles fighting a flock of man-eating birds.

Doric

Ionic

Twenty "flutes" (grooves)

Doric has a simple saucer shape on its capital (top).

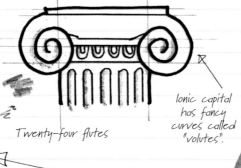

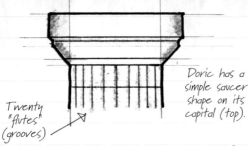
The Acropolis is the hill the Parthenon stands on. Ancient cities often settled on high ground to defend against invasion.

DORIC AND IONIC COLUMNS

At 10.4 m (34 ft) tall, 49 Doric columns line the outside of the temple, with 17 on each flank. These columns bulge in the middle and narrow towards the top, so that from a distance they look straight. Four Ionic columns stand in the opisthodomos — they are slimmer and more elaborate.

Twenty-four flutes

Ionic capital has fancy curves called "volutes".

STATUE OF ATHENA

The original wooden statue was covered in ivory "flesh", with a removable *peplos* (robe) of gold. Destroyed long ago, it is thought to have stood at more than 12 m (39 ft). There are many other statues of Athena around the city, such as this one from the Academy of Arts.

HORSE OF SELENE

The pediment (triangular roof end) on the east side of the entrance had carvings depicting Athena being born fully grown from her father Zeus' skull. This horse witnessed the strange birth – no wonder it looks surprised!

N-A-A-A-Y!

Golden oldie shines anew

5 SEPTEMBER 2002

A golden goddess has been unveiled in the city of Nashville, USA. The copy of the Athena statue was sculptured by Alan LeQuire in 1990, but the gold-leaf covering was not applied until this year. The statue towers inside a full-scale replica of the Parthenon, built in 1897. In her right palm Athena holds a winged statue of Nike, the Greek goddess of victory.

KIDNAPPED!

The Parthenon was decorated with 92 metopes – rectangular blocks carved with scenes from mythical battles. This poor girl is being carried off by a centaur (a half-man, half-horse creature).

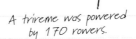

THE GREAT PANATHENAEA

Every four years, in Athena's birthday month of Hekatombion, Athenians held a five-day festival. Noble girls wove the statue a giant *peplos* (robe), others sacrificed animals, and there was a great procession up to the Parthenon. The frieze around the outside of the *naos* (main room) shows 360 citizens and cavalry in this parade.

I've discovered that Athena's birthday was in the month of Hekatombion ("100 oxen") on the Athenian calendar, around July–August. The festival seems to have been one of the most important in the Ancient Greek world.

So I've decided to draw the Parthenon as it was during one of these festivals, in Athens' Golden Age. I'm quite close to solving the riddle, too. "Marbled" makes me think that it's part of the building...

TRIREME SHIP

The Parthenon cost 469 silver talents to build. The trireme, the most advanced warship of the time, only cost one talent.

A trireme was powered by 170 rowers.

TIMELINE

480 BCE
Persians destroy original Acropolis.

431–404
Athens at war with other Greek city-states.

520
Byzantines convert Parthenon to a Christian church.

1688
Small mosque built inside the Parthenon's burnt-out ruins.

1205
Parthenon converted to a Catholic cathedral — the Notre Dame d'Athènes.

1801
Ottoman sultan lets Lord Elgin remove bits of the ruins. Some marble slabs are sawn in half for transportation to England.

447
Construction of the Parthenon begins.

433
Sculptures are completed.

432
Structural work is completed.

5th century CE
Statue of Athena is looted and taken to Constantinople where it is later destroyed.

1687
Venetians fire mortar shell at Parthenon. It explodes and burns for two days.

Today
Pollution corrodes the marble surface causing irreparable damage. Conservation groups attempt repairs.

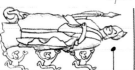

Inside the Parthenon

1. The huge cult statue of Athena dominates the temple's inner sanctuary (naos).

2. A shallow pool of water or oil lies in front of the statue. The pool reflects light from the doorway up onto the statue to increase its visual impact.

3. A priestess leads the religious ceremony.

4. The citizens form a procession along the Panathenaic Way, bringing gifts and animals for sacrifice. Only native-born Athenians are allowed to enter the Acropolis.

5. Goats, pigs, and oxen are sacrificed on the Great Altar of Athena. Some parts of the meat are burned as an offering to the goddess.

6. Another temple, called the Erechtheion, stands to the side of the Parthenon, and is also dedicated to Athena.

7. A second statue of Athena stands outside the Parthenon. Known as Athena Promachos ("Athena who fights in the front line"), the bronze statue shows the goddess with a shield and holding a spear.

8. Doric columns line the exterior walls of the building. Above the columns runs the frieze, decorated with carvings.

9. The steep walls of the Acropolis rise 150 m (512 ft) above sea level.

10. Many statues of gods and goddesses stand on pedestals, painted in bright, gaudy colours.

The Colosseum

Dear Steve,

These ruins aren't huge, they're COLOSSAL. This certainly wasn't built in one day. Many wild parties were held here — sometimes, it seemed like a zoo! Waiting for a riddle? Let the (word) games begin.

Eighty spots where great crowds spew,
But some aren't for the likes of you!

I hope it's adding up.

Jack

Stephen Biesty
c/o The Attica Inn,
Athens,
Greece

1.30

THE ROMANS

Ancient Roman society was organized in a hierarchy. The emperor ruled at the top, free-born citizens came next, and slaves were the bottom class. Slaves were the possessions of their masters, who had the power of life and death over them.

Senator

Slave

Citizen

Completed in 80 CE, the Colosseum was Ancient Rome's ultimate entertainment venue, seating up to 50,000 people. Reigning emperors hosted epic spectacles here — gladiators fought to the death and warriors sparred with wild animals.

A TALE OF TWO EMPERORS

Construction of the Colosseum was overseen by the emperor Vespasian. After his death in 79 CE, his son Titus became emperor. In 80 CE, Titus marked the opening of the Colosseum with 100 days of games.

COLOSSUS OF NERO

Historians think the name *Colosseum* came from the Colossus – a 37-m- (121-ft-) high bronze statue of Nero that stood nearby.

I knew I was headed to Rome when Jack referred to the old saying "Rome wasn't built in a day". And when he wrote "COLOSSAL" I knew he had to be referring to the Colosseum. There were certainly lots of games held here, and many of them involved exotic animals so it would have seemed like a zoo.

Eighty spots where great crowds spew? Surely Jack doesn't mean real vomit. Gross!

STADIUM SEATING

The Colosseum's seating structure mirrored the Roman class system. Senators sat around the emperor on the podium — some of their names are still carved in the stones.

Standing room only at the top for women and the lower classes.

The third tier was for citizens. The richer they were, the lower down they sat.

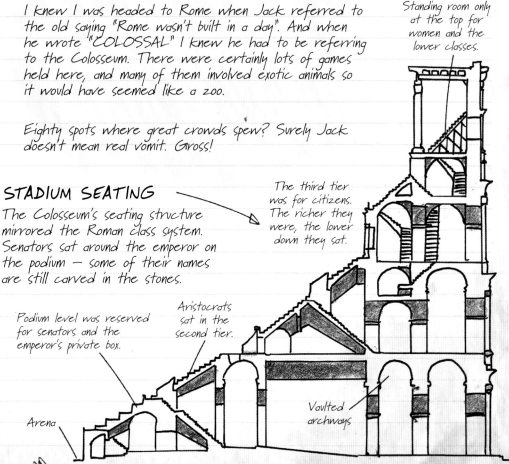

Podium level was reserved for senators and the emperor's private box.

Aristocrats sat in the second tier.

Arena

Vaulted archways

ARENA FIGHTS

Professional fighters called gladiators fought to the death in the Colosseum arena. While many were slaves or prisoners of war, some gladiators were free citizens seeking fame and fortune.

Eighty arched entrances — four exclusively for the use of royalty and dignitaries — line the exterior of the Colosseum. They were called vomitoria, from a Latin word meaning "rapid discharge".

TRAPDOOR SURPRISE

During contests, exotic animals were unleashed into the arena from trapdoors set into the floor. Specialist fighters known as venatores battled beasts including lions, boars, and crocodiles. These creatures were shipped from Africa for the contests.

A standing area was added for women and the lowest classes.

Sometimes the arena was filled with water to host naval battles.

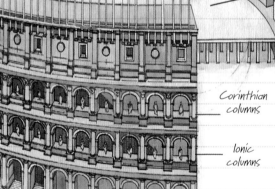

Corinthian columns

Ionic columns

Doric columns

ARENA AND BELOW

All entertainment took place in the arena. Sand covered the wooden floor to soak the blood spilled in the many contests and executions. Underneath lay a maze of tunnels called the hypogeum. While it was a storeroom for props, it was also backstage for warriors and beasts waiting to be thrust into battle.

COLUMNS

The entire amphitheatre is ringed with arcades of different style columns. Doric columns are wider on the bottom, Ionic columns have a scroll design on top, and Corinthian columns are topped with a leaf design.

Corinthian column

34

WRACK AND RUIN

Over the centuries, the Colosseum has been damaged by a number of large earthquakes. Its stones were stripped to build grand churches, palaces, and public buildings. Restoration work began in the 19th century.

Emperor Trajan

Trajan's games sound pretty gruesome to me. They'll make a good subject for my illustration, but I'm glad entertainment is less gory these days.

"Eighty spots where great crowds spew." Now, I'm pretty sure Jack isn't talking about vomit. But I think I know what he's hinting at.

"But some aren't for the likes of you." The likes of me?! Well, I guess this place did entertain many important emperors and dignitaries in its time. But what's wrong with being an illustrator, eh?

TRAJAN'S TRIUMPH

In 107 CE, the emperor Trajan celebrated Rome's victory in the wars against the kingdom of Dacia with games. Around 9,000 gladiators were killed in the festivities at the Colosseum, which went on for 117 days.

Trajan's Column commemorates Rome's victory. The carvings on it depict the battles of the Dacian Wars.

TIMELINE

Around **70** CE
Emperor Vespasian begins construction.

80
Emperor Titus opens Colosseum with 100-day inaugural games

443
Major earthquake hits Colosseum. Restoration takes 50 years.

1349
Major earthquake collapses much of the south side.

1300s–1600s
Colosseum serves as quarry. Many of the stones are plundered.

1807
Facade of building is reinforced with triangular brick wedges.

217
Lightning strikes and fire destroys upper wooden levels. Restoration takes 20 years.

425
Last known gladiator games are recorded

523
Last known animal hunts are recorded.

1200
Colosseum becomes a fortress and castle.

1749
Pope Benedict XIV deems Colosseum a sacred Christian site.

Today
More than 2.5 million visitors annually.

Inside the Colosseum

1. Large awnings, known as velaria, are pulled across the amphitheatre to shade the audience from the sun.

2. Vomitoria (corridored entrances) let the stadium fill up in just 15 minutes.

3. The emperor's box is at the bottom of the north side of the arena.

4. Trapdoors built into the arena floor hide wild beasts and warriors.

5. Main gate to the arena where gladiators are welcomed by cheering (and jeering) crowds.

6. Exotic animals in cages, ready to be released into the arena.

7. The hypogeum beneath the arena has a series of lifts to transport people, props, and creatures through the trapdoors in the arena floor.

8. An injured gladiator is patched up by doctors.

9. Different types of gladiator have different weapons. Retarius has a net and trident (three-pronged spear).

10. In 107, the emperor Trajan holds extravagant and bloodthirsty games that last 117 days.

Notre Dame Cathedral

Standing majestically on a small island on the River Seine, Notre Dame de Paris is one of the world's earliest Gothic cathedrals. In 1163, Pope Alexander III laid its foundation stone. Over the next 170 years, it was a huge construction site of stones and towering scaffolds.

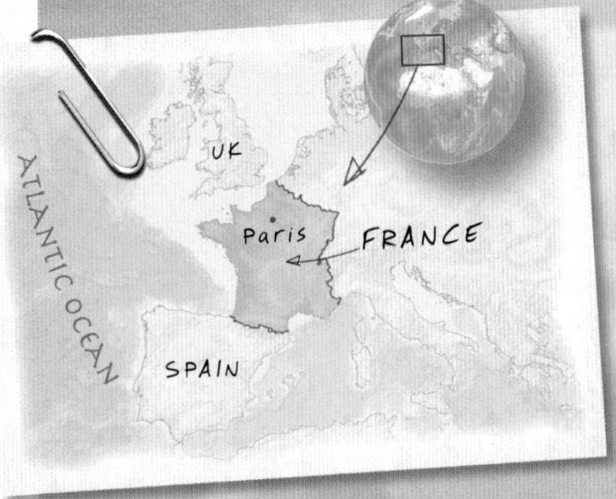

ATLANTIC OCEAN

UK

Paris

FRANCE

SPAIN

Bonjour Steve,

I'm in the City of Light — and what illuminating advice do I have? Remember to stand up straight! There's just one hunchback lurking in these parts. Okay, he is a work of fiction, but this sacred spot is real. Does this riddle ring any bells for you?

Side by side, these crowned men stand. "Off with their heads!" is the people's command.

Jack

1.50

Stephen Biesty
c/o Caesar's Palace B&B,
Rome,
Italy

GRUESOME GROTESQUES

Sculpted, spooky-looking creatures called grotesques form part of Notre Dame's stonework. They were designed to ward off evil. Some, known as gargoyles, function as rainspouts, spitting water from the roof.

KEY FEATURES OF GOTHIC ARCHITECTURE

❶ Pointed, instead of rounded, arches. These are found on the ceilings and over doorways and windows.

❷ Sharp spires reaching high up into the sky.

❸ Stained-glass windows depicting images of the saints or stories from the Bible.

❹ Flying buttresses — external arches that support the weight of the roof.

LIFE IN MEDIEVAL FRANCE

At the time Notre Dame was built, France was ruled by a king. The king, nobility, and Church were very rich, but most people were poor. Disaster struck when the Black Death arrived in Europe in 1348. The plague killed one-third of the population - both rich and poor.

When Jack wrote "bonjour" (French for "hello") and mentioned a "City of Light" in his postcard, a light bulb of my own lit up. Where else could he possibly mean but Paris?

Once I arrived, I did what any tourist would do and scaled the Eiffel Tower (well, I took the lift). From this vantage point, I scoured Paris through my binoculars. Lo and behold, there was the "sacred spot" — Notre Dame Cathedral.

Hunchback? Work of fiction? That has to mean Victor Hugo's famous book, The Hunchback of Notre Dame. Now I know I'm in the right place.

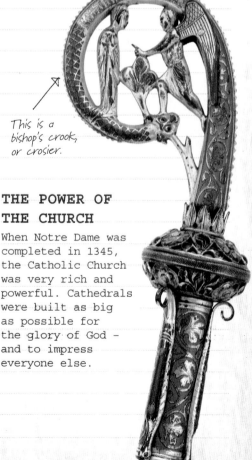

This is a bishop's crook, or crosier.

HOW IT WAS BUILT

Many architects worked on Notre Dame over its 170-year construction, bringing different styles to the cathedral. Thousands of craftspeople - including carpenters, blacksmiths, glassmakers, and sculptors - helped piece it together, while teams of labourers moved stones from quarries.

THE POWER OF THE CHURCH

When Notre Dame was completed in 1345, the Catholic Church was very rich and powerful. Cathedrals were built as big as possible for the glory of God - and to impress everyone else.

THE WEST FRONT

The west front of the cathedral stretches upwards in three layers. Above the portals (doorways) is a layer of stained-glass windows, and above them sit the two bell towers.

North tower

South tower

Known as "Emmanuel", the bell inside the south tower weighs 13 tonnes.

The Galerie des Chimères bridges the north and south tower. This is where the cathedral's gargoyles roost.

Built before 1250, much of the original glass in the west rose window remains.

The Kings Gallery contains 28 statues representing kings from the Bible. The original figures were beheaded in the French Revolution (1789–1799).

The Portal of the Virgin shows the coronation of the Virgin Mary.

"Side by side, these crowned men stand." Is Jack talking about a line of royalty here? "Off with their heads!" During the French Revolution, many statues were defaced. Now I just need to find out if any royal ones were decapitated.

ROSE WINDOW

Surprisingly, the rose window isn't named after the sweet-smelling flower. Instead, it comes from the Old French word roue, which means "wheel".

It's astounding how long this place took to build. I think that is what I'll base my illustration on.

PORTALS

The stone carvings around the three portals on the west front retell stories from the Bible.

NAPOLEON'S CORONATION

On 2 December 1804, Napoleon Bonaparte crowned himself the first emperor of France in a lavish ceremony in Notre Dame Cathedral. Bonaparte was a leader of the French Revolution, during which the king and other royals were executed.

FRANCE: Paris, Notre D

TIMELINE

1160
Bishop Maurice de Sully orders the original cathedral to be demolished.

1163
Cornerstone laid for Notre Dame de Paris and construction begins.

1225
West front completed.

1345
Cathedral construction completed.

1558
Mary I of Scotland marries the king of France's son.

1804
Napoleon Bonaparte crowned emperor.

1831
Hunchback of Notre Dame published.

1920
Joan of Arc created a saint in Notre Dame ceremony.

Today
Notre Dame attracts more than 12 million visitors each year.

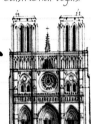

NOVEL INSPIRATION

In 1831, Victor Hugo wrote the novel *The Hunchback of Notre Dame*. The bell-ringing adventures of the fictional hunchback, Quasimodo, have inspired a number of films and stage musicals.

INSIDE THE CATHEDRAL

Notre Dame is still used as a Catholic place of worship. The cathedral is also a top tourist attraction in Paris. Visitors can climb the 422 narrow steps to the top of the south tower.

South tower houses the Emmanuel bell.

The spire soars to a height of 90 m (50 ft).

The flying buttresses span 15 m (50 ft).

The treasury houses the cathedral's religious treasures, including ancient manuscripts.

The west rose window depicts the Virgin Mary in rich shards of red and blue glass.

The Kings Gallery features 28 Bible kings gazing down on the crowds below.

All road distances in France are measured from "Point Zero" in the square in front of the cathedral.

The main vault (ceiling) inside the cathedral is 34 m (112 ft) high.

The south rose window is 13 m (43 ft) across and depicts Christ surrounded by saints.

Inside Notre Dame Cathedral

1. It is the year 1230, and Notre Dame towers over Paris, symbolizing the power of the Church.

2. The vault (arched ceiling) soars to a height of 34 m (112 ft).

3. Small groups of builders add finishing touches to the flying buttresses, designed to support the weight of the vault and prevent the walls from buckling.

4. Inside, architects and officials survey the building's progress.

5. Stained-glass windows let light filter in from above.

6. Internal walls are painted white. A vivid red mortar is used between the bricks, with saints and angels depicted above the arches in glowing yellow.

7. Painters and craftsmen climb scaffolding to reach the upper walls and ceilings of the cathedral.

8. The stained-glass west rose window spans 10 m (32 ft).

9. Groups of stone gargoyles roost along the cathedral's gutters.

10. There are two aisles on either side of the nave (central area), separated by pointed arches.

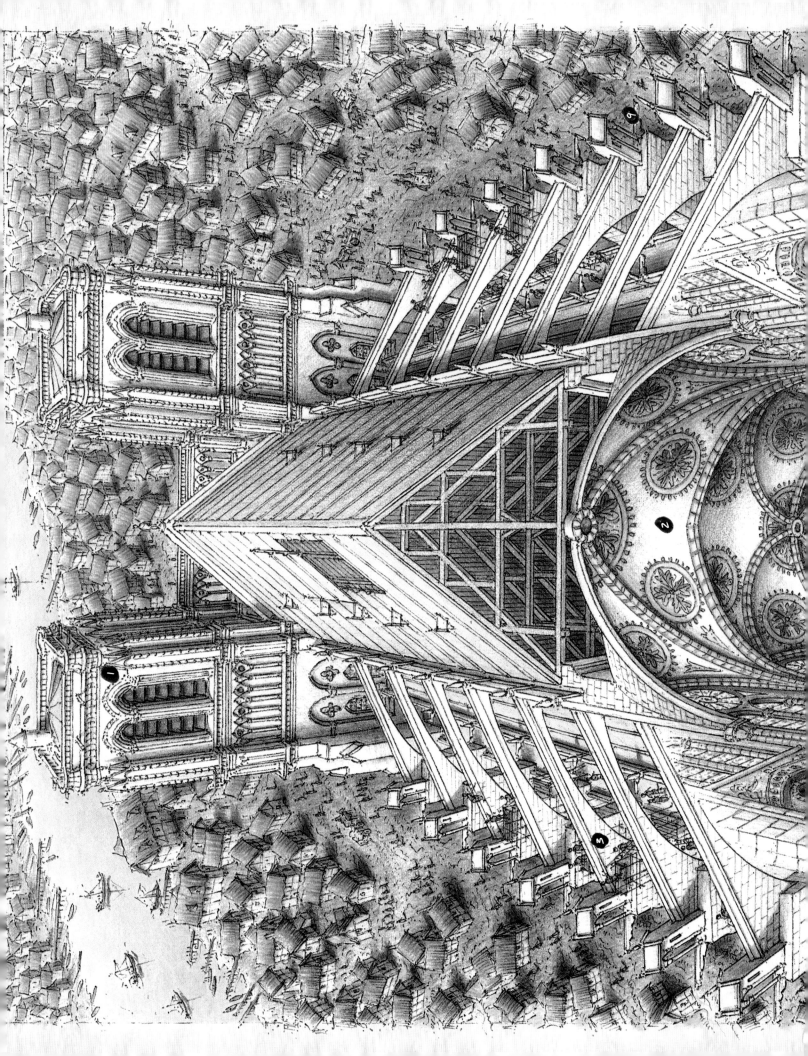

Globe Theatre

NORTH SEA

UNITED KINGDOM

ATLANTIC OCEAN

London

EUROPE

Dear Steve,

You've trotted the globe, yet there's another one to explore. Outer space, you say? Now, let's not be too dramatic! Next up, your riddle. What is it to be — or not to be? That is the question.

Up in smoke! Which king was he who stood on stage in front of thee?

Hope it goes off with a BANG!

Jack

Stephen Biesty
L'Hôtel des
Beaux-Arts,
Paris,
France

The Globe Theatre was built in 1599 on the south bank of the River Thames in London. The playwright William Shakespeare was one of the building's owners and many of his famous plays were staged there. The Globe was dismantled in 1644, but in 1997 a reconstruction was built just metres from the original site.

THE GLOBE THEATRE

The original Globe Theatre was home to the Lord Chamberlain's Men, a company of actors that included William Shakespeare. In 1599, the men built the Globe using timber stripped – and, it was argued, stolen – from their previous playhouse, the Theatre. The Globe closed in 1642 and most impressions of it today are based on a surviving 1596 sketch of rival London theatre, the Swan.

ELIZABETHAN ERA

England was a hive of culture and commerce during the reign of Queen Elizabeth I (1558–1603). Attending the theatre was a popular pastime for both the wealthy and the working class. The most celebrated works were by playwrights Christopher Marlowe and William Shakespeare.

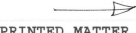

PRINTED MATTER

Books known as "quatros" are the earliest records of Shakespeare's plays. Usually, publishers printed 800 copies of a play for its first edition. In Shakespeare's lifetime, 18 of his plays were printed. It is believed that his first quarto was the tragedy *Titus Andronicus* in 1594.

THE MOST LAmentable Romaine Tragedie of Titus Andronicus:

As it was Plaide by the Right Honourable the Earle of *Darbie*, Earle of *Pembrooke*, and Earle of *Suſſex* their Seruants.

LONDON,
Printed by Iohn Danter, and are to be sold by *Edward White* & *Thomas Millington*, at the little North doore of Paules at the ſigne of the Gunne,
1594.

Jack's postcard made me laugh. I might be adventurous, but travelling to outer space? I forgot to pack my moon boots! I knew "another globe" had to mean something else...

With the quote "To be or not to be? That is the question" there was only one answer – William Shakespeare, of course!

It might not be the original theatre, but this reconstruction of Shakespeare's Globe certainly makes me feel like I've stepped back to Elizabethan times.

TIMELINE

1594
The Lord Chamberlain's Men are named after the title of their patron, Henry Carey.

1598
Timber is taken from the Theatre to build the Globe.

1599
The Globe Theatre opens.

1600
The Lord Chamberlains' Men are the most famous theatrical company in London.

1603
Queen Elizabeth I dies and James I becomes king. The Lord Chamberlain's Men become the King's Men.

1613
Cannon misfires during a performance of Shakespeare's Henry VIII. Globe burns to the ground.

1614
Globe rebuilt with a tiled rather than thatched roof.

1616
William Shakespeare dies.

1642
Globe closed down by a religious group called the Puritans.

1644
Globe demolished to build housing.

1997
A reconstruction of the original Globe Theatre opens in London.

45

THE RECONSTRUCTION

The modern reconstruction used archaeological evidence to be as faithful to the original as possible. It was the first building in London to be allowed a thatched roof since the Great Fire destroyed much of the city in 1666.

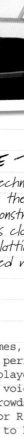

TIMBER FRAME

The same building techniques were used for both the original and the reconstruction. A timber frame was clad with wattle and daub, a latticework of thin timber coated with layers of plaster.

THE PLAYERS

In Elizabethan times, all roles - male and female - were performed by male actors known as "players". They needed loud and strident voices to be heard above the noisy crowds of more than 3,000 people. Actor Richard Burbage (left) is thought to have starred in all of Shakespeare's plays.

I went to see a production of Hamlet at the modern Globe — it was amazing! I wish I'd paid the extra money for a cushion though, those benches were hard.

"Up in smoke!" Well, I do know that smoke was sometimes released from the trapdoor as a special effect.

"Off with a bang." Hmmm, actually, Jack might be referring to cannon fire. When the Globe burnt down in 1613 things certainly would have gone off with a bang! Imagine the mayhem — Shakespeare's crowds were unruly at the best of times. I wonder if the audience ever got to see the rest of the play. I think I'll choose that incident to illustrate in my reconstruction.

Hazelnuts were a popular theatre snack, with the shells lining the floor.

OUCH!
You wouldn't want to walk over these with a hole in your shoe!

A sprinkler system was installed to prevent fire destroying the modern theatre.

Electric lighting means evening performances are possible.

People on the hard benches can hire a cushion for greater comfort.

As in the past, the cheaper tickets are standing only.

THE GLOBE TODAY

Today, Shakespeare's Globe Theatre is a popular tourist attraction as well as an active playhouse. Each year, more than 750,000 visitors attend plays and see exhibitions on Shakespearean costume, music, and special effects.

If a performance was poor, actors sometimes found themselves pelted with rotten tomatoes.

B - A - N - G!

SHAKESPEARE'S ROLE
As well as being the Globe's playwright, William Shakespeare was also an actor, taking on minor roles. He part-owned the theatre as a "sharer", which meant he had a big stake in writing successful plays.

UP IN SMOKE

On 29 June 1613, the Globe Theatre burned down after cannon fire ignited the thatched roof during a performance of Henry VIII. Rebuilt the same year, it was torn down in 1644 to make way for housing. Around this time, a strict religious group known as the Puritans closed all the playhouses in London.

Small cannons were used for sound effects during plays, for example to herald the entrance of important characters.

ENGLAND: London, Gl

47

Inside the Globe Theatre

1 Cannon in the eaves of the stage canopy is used as a sound effect. It misfires and a blaze ignites.

2 Dry thatched roof becomes tinder and feeds the raging fire.

3 Only the wealthiest can afford a seat in the expensive top gallery,

4 but hundreds of poor people are crammed into the pit.

5 The audience spots the fire spreading and begins to panic.

6 Hawkers sell snack food to the hungry crowd.

7 Three doors on stage lead to the backstage area or "tiring house".

4 On stage, players perform a scene from Henry VIII. Littered about the stage are sheepskins. In the play King Henry VIII mingles among his court by disguising himself as a shepherd.

8 Columns support the stage canopy, known as the "heavens".

9 Seating galleries are accessed from stairs outside the theatre.

10 The admission takings are stowed in boxes backstage, in the "box office".

Empire State Building

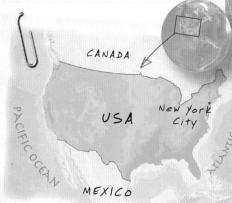

CANADA

USA

New York City

PACIFIC OCEAN

ATLANTIC OCEAN

MEXICO

When it was opened in 1931, the Empire State Building was the tallest structure on Earth. Today, it is the tallest building in New York City, soaring 443.2 m (1,453.75 ft) to its highest point — a lightning rod.

The building opened during the Great Depression and was nicknamed the "Empty State Building" because so much of its office space remained vacant. Today, many of its 1,000 tenants are TV stations, who broadcast directly from the building.

DEAR STEVE,

HERE I AM, STANDING IN A SYMBOL OF A MODERN EMPIRE. I FOUND MYSELF A BIG APPLE — WITHOUT AN ORCHARD IN SIGHT! BUT, FROM THIS LOFTY HEIGHT, I CAN LOOK DOWN ON ONE OF THE WORLD'S GREATEST CITIES. TO SOLVE THIS RIDDLE, STEVE, YOU'LL NEED TO THINK ON YOUR FEET.

SCALING HEIGHTS TO SAVE SORE FEET, THESE BOXES ROCKET FROM THE STREET.

Jack

1.10

STEPHEN BIESTY
c/o SAVOY HOTEL,
LONDON,
UNITED KINGDOM

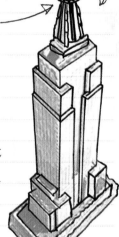

The 1920s and 1930s were the heyday of airship travel.

Blimps were to be tethered here! Got a lasso?

Passengers would have disembarked along a walkway more than 441 m (1,447 ft) up.

Tower to top them all is a really tall story

31 JANUARY 1931

With more than 3,400 construction staff working around the clock through weekends and holidays, the Empire State Building is rising at an astonishing 4.5 storeys a week. Financier John J. Raskob is determined his 102-storey tower will beat rival skyscrapers, the Chrysler Building and 40 Wall Street. Will the Empire State Building be the tallest of the crop?

DOCK SHOCK

The mast was designed to moor blimps (airships), but the plan was abandoned in September 1931 when a docking blimp almost turned over, gushing its water ballast (stabilizing weight) over several city blocks.

I've asked a few New Yorkers why it is called the "Big Apple"? Some say it is a nickname horse-racing jockeys gave the city in the 1920s, while others argue jazz musicians called it that in the 30s. Confused? Maybe that is a riddle I can't solve.

Jack's postcard was interesting. When I saw the word "empire" I quickly realized he was talking about the Empire State Building. I could hardly miss it, not even in a city of eight million people!

It's amazing that the Empire State Building was built in just one year and 45 days.

"Think on your feet." That's something I've had to do on this quest. I'm getting blisters! I'll certainly be taking the elevator to get to the top.

THE BREADLINE

The Empire State Building was built during the Great Depression, a worldwide economic slump triggered by the 1929 Wall Street stock exchange crash in New York City. Banks, factories, and shops closed, and many people had to queue for food at charity-run soup kitchens.

SHOOTING SKYWARDS

The building tapers inwards in a "setback" formation to satisfy a US law of the time preventing skyscrapers from casting large shadows over the city.

102nd-floor observatory

86th-floor observatory

Coloured floodlighting of the top 30 floors marks special and seasonal events.

73 high-speed elevators travel at up to 366 m (1,200 ft) a minute.

Despite my sore feet, I decided to see for myself just how many steps there are from the 102nd floor back down to the lobby. There are 1,860!

Next time, I'm sticking to the elevator. I certainly had quite a few of those to choose from.

I think I'll draw the skyscraper as it looked when it was officially opened in May 1931. Just need to collect a few more facts about it first...

BIRD'S-EYE VIEW

In clear weather, views from the Empire State Building stretch 130 km (80 miles) across four states. If all 73 elevators are busy, there are 1,575 steps from the lobby to the 86th-floor observation deck, with another 285 steps to reach the 102nd floor.

Ten million bricks were used to line the whole building.

Sandwich space between the floors houses the wiring, pipes, and cables.

The framework is made from 54,430 tonnes of steel and was built in 23 weeks.

More than 200 steel and concrete piles support the 331,122-tonne building.

A GRAND ENTRANCE

The entrance lobby is an imposing three storeys of lavish granite and marble. It is decorated with brushed stainless steel and bronze medallions commemorating the many craftspeople responsible for building it.

TIMELINE

1930
Excavation begins at the former Waldorf-Astoria Hotel site on 22 January.

1931
Official opening on 1 May. President Roosevelt lights the building from Washington DC.

1945
In heavy fog on 28 July, a US B-25 bomber plane crashes into the 79th floor. Ten civilians and 3 servicemen are killed, with another man later dying from his injuries.

1964
Artist Andy Warhol films the Empire State Building in one still shot across eight whole hours. He calls this silent film "Empire".

1972
At 110 storeys, the World Trade Center's Tower 1 becomes New York's (and the world's) tallest building.

1978
The first Empire State Run-up is held — an annual race to run up the 1,575 steps to the 86th floor.

1986
The Empire State Building is recognized as a National Historic Landmark.

2007
The skyscraper is named America's favourite structure in an American Institute of Architects poll.

2001
After the World Trade Center is destroyed on 11 September, the Empire State Building is again New York's tallest building.

HOLLYWOOD ICON

The Empire State Building has featured in around 100 movies. The most famous of these is the 1933 film *King Kong*, in which a giant ape climbs the tower.

13 KILLED AS PLANE RAMS 79TH FLOOR

28 JULY 1945

At 9.49 am, a US B-25 bomber crashed into the Empire State Building, tragically killing 10 office employees and three airmen. One War Relief Services employee is fighting for his life, with another 26 people suffering injuries. Traffic control at New York's La Guardia airport reported that the plane became lost in heavy fog.

RACE WITH CHRYSLER

John J. Raskob was the arch business rival of car manufacturer Walter Chrysler. Throughout construction, both men battled to make their skyscraper the tallest. Raskob won by adding the blimp mast at the top of the Empire State Building.

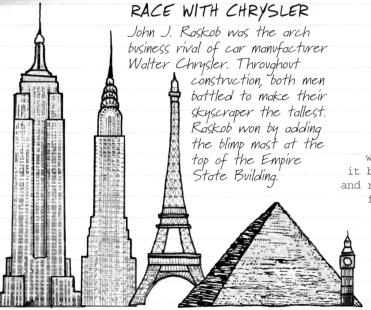

Empire State Building, NYC, USA	Chrysler Building, NYC, USA	Eiffel Tower, Paris, France	Great Pyramid Giza, Egypt	Big Ben London, UK
443.2 m (1,453 ft)	319 m (1,046 ft)	300 m (984 ft)	138 m (453 ft)	91 m (299 ft)

TRANSMITTER

When the mooring mast was abandoned, the "hat" on top of the Empire State Building became a transmission tower. Covered with antennae, it broadcasts TV and radio across five states.

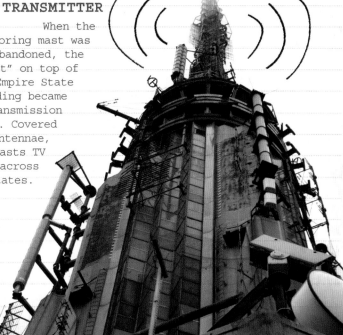

Inside the Empire State Building

1. The 86th-floor observation deck provides panoramic views over New York City.

2. The cavernous three-storey lobby is lined with marble panels.

3. At the grand opening, hordes of press and spectators gather in the lobby, eager to rocket to the top of the world's tallest building.

4. Escalators and elevators take visitors to the upper levels.

5. The structure tapers inwards in a layered "setback" formation.

6. A large metal panel depicts the building as the centre of both New York City and the universe.

7. 6,500 windows sit flush with the building's limestone facade.

8. Ten million bricks were used in the building's construction.

9. The skyscraper is in the ultra-modern Art Deco style, characterized by bold shapes and patterns of straight lines and curves.

10. Much of the office space went unrented when the building first opened during the Great Depression.

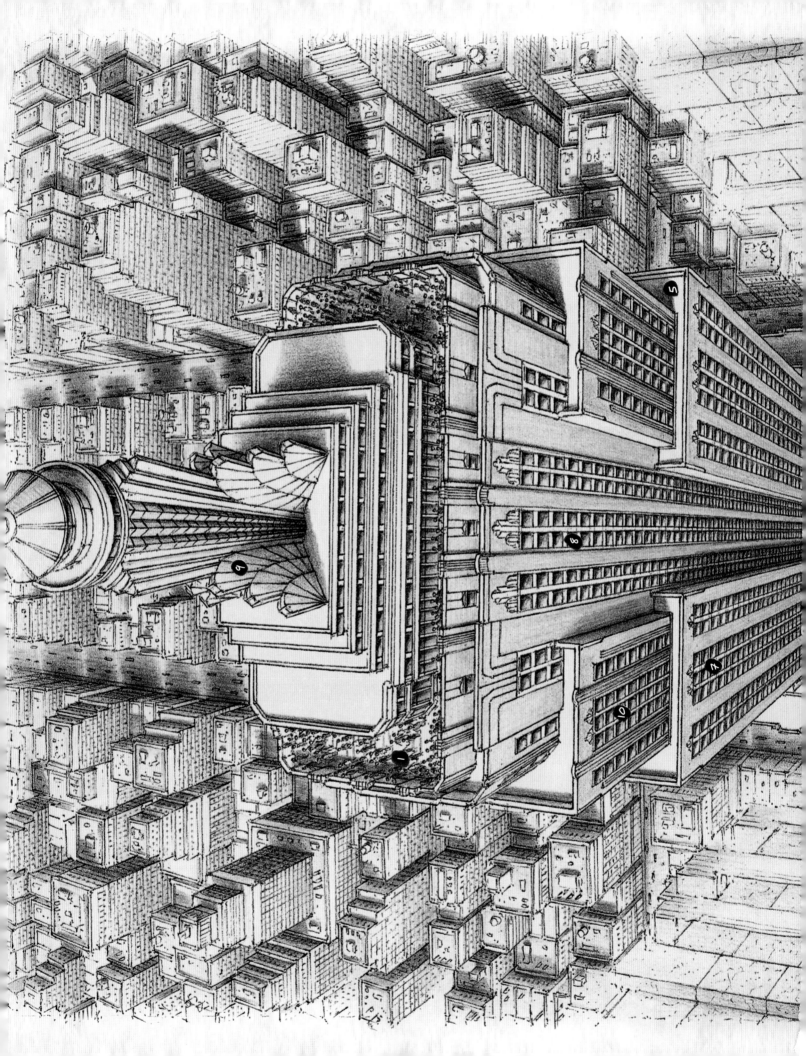

Temple of the Inscriptions

Shrouded by the lush forest of Mexico's Sierra de Palenque mountains, the ruins of Palenque hide many secrets. Abandoned around 900, the former city-state is an archaeological marvel, filled with architecture, sculptures, and stone carvings from the ancient Mayan civilization. Rising from the mist is the majestic Temple of Inscriptions, tomb of King Pakal the Great (603–683).

Archaeologists believe that about 500 buildings remain buried in Palenque's foothills.

USA

MEXICO

GULF OF MEXICO

PACIFIC OCEAN

Palenque

Dear Steve,

May another adventure begin. This time, go south. Uncover a spot where a king forever sleeps, surrounded by riddles. Surprisingly, he made his own bed. Puzzled? Well, here is another riddle to add to the bunch.

Told in three parts, a story unfolds, For now we can count the secrets it holds.

Are you still counting?

Jack

Stephen Biesty,
c/o The Waldorf
Astoria,
Park Avenue,
New York, NY,
USA

This one was tricky! To "go south" from New York could have meant any number of places. When I saw "MAYAN" on the postcard, I was off to Mexico, home of the Mayan civilization.

To say someone "forever sleeps" may mean they are dead.

"Made his own bed?" Pakal built the Temple of Inscriptions as his tomb. A bit odd, but that's how things must have been done in those days.

PUZZLING PLAQUES

In the Mayan language, written information was pieced together in a series of pictures or "glyphs". The Temple of Inscriptions is named after three hieroglyphic plaques that stand inside its entrance.

Mayan tomb uncovered

15 JUNE 1952

A 1,300-year-old Mayan tomb has been unearthed in the jungle at Palenque, Mexico. The tomb was found by archaeologist Alberto Ruz Lhuillier and is believed to contain the coffin of Mayan king Pakal the Great.

"For the first time in more than 1,000 years, human eyes saw the carved sarcophagus lid of a great ruler," said Ruz Lhuillier.

Excavations began in 1949, after Lhuillier found a mismatching stone in the top floor of the Temple of Inscriptions. Beneath this lay a rubble-filled stairway leading to Pakal's tomb.

PAKAL THE GREAT

Pakal the Great was born in 603. He became Palenque's king at the age of 12. After his death in 683, the Mayan people revered him as a god.

CRACKING THE GLYPH

Archaeologists are still trying to decipher the 617 glyphs carved into the three plaques. Pakal's name translates to "hand shield". His glyph can be broken into five parts:

Mah K'ina — title of respect

Shield icon — meaning "Pakal"

Syllable "pa"

Syllable "ka"

Syllable "la" — together, the three right-side pictures phonetically form "Pakal".

TIMELINE

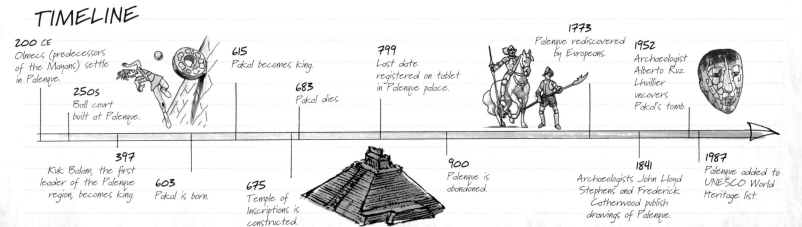

200 CE
Olmecs (predecessors of the Mayans) settle in Palenque.

250s
Ball court built at Palenque.

397
Kuk Balam, the first leader of the Palenque region, becomes king.

603
Pakal is born.

615
Pakal becomes king.

683
Pakal dies.

675
Temple of Inscriptions is constructed.

799
Last date registered on tablet in Palenque palace.

900
Palenque is abandoned.

1773
Palenque rediscovered by Europeans.

1841
Archaeologists John Lloyd Stephens and Frederick Catherwood publish drawings of Palenque.

1952
Archaeologist Alberto Ruz Lhuillier uncovers Pakal's tomb.

1987
Palenque added to UNESCO World Heritage list.

STAIRWAY TO THE TOMB

Beneath the temple floor, Lhuillier's team revealed a staircase of 66 steps. At its base was a room scattered with the skeletons of people sacrificed in Pakal's funeral ceremony. A triangular door guarded the 7-m- (23-ft-) high chamber containing the king's coffin. The vaulted crypt was cloaked in glittering stalagmites and stalactites (caused by water dripping from the limestone rock) that had formed over hundreds of years.

MEXICO: Palenque, Temple

THE ARCHAEOLOGICAL SITE

Today, Palenque stretches across 65 sq km (25 sq miles). It is estimated that less than 35 per cent of the ancient city-state has been unearthed from the thick jungle.

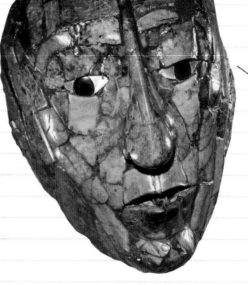

Many historians think Pakal's well-preserved teeth belonged to someone much younger than 80.

"Told in three parts, a story unfolds." Very cryptic, Jack. I guess all stories have three parts — a beginning, a middle, and an end. I wonder how THIS story will end.

"We can count the secrets it holds." I have been looking around for "secrets", and the Temple of Inscriptions hides many astonishing surprises — especially Pakal's tomb.

The temple takes its name from its three plaques carved with inscriptions. This has got to be the story in three parts that Jack is referring to. Now I just have to figure out how many "secrets" are to be found there.

PAKAL'S REMAINS

When Pakal's tomb was unearthed in 1952, his remains were covered in beaded necklaces and strips of cotton. Upon his skull rested an exquisitely crafted jade death mask. Following Mayan rituals, a string of jade had been placed in Pakal's mouth to symbolize "breath" in the afterlife.

There were thirteen heavens in Mayan mythology, each with its own god

Earthly life was at all times connected to the heavens above and the underworld below.

Xibalba means "place of phantoms". The road to it was steep and dangerous.

PAKAL'S SARCOPHAGUS

A "World Tree" was carved into the lid of Pakal's sarcophagus. The inscriptions described the king's life, family, and journey after death. Inside, Pakal's body had been carefully preserved.

THE WORLD TREE

Pakal is shown falling along a route connecting his earthly life as ruler over Palenque, the heavens above, and an underworld known as "Xibalba". According to Mayan beliefs, it was there that Pakal would be reborn into a new life.

PALENQUE COMPLEX

At its peak, it is thought that Palenque housed more than 6,000 people. During the reign of Pakal the Great, the city experienced a boom time of building palaces, temples, and elaborate tombs. However, it wasn't all hard work — the pitch for an ancient ball game was discovered in excavations.

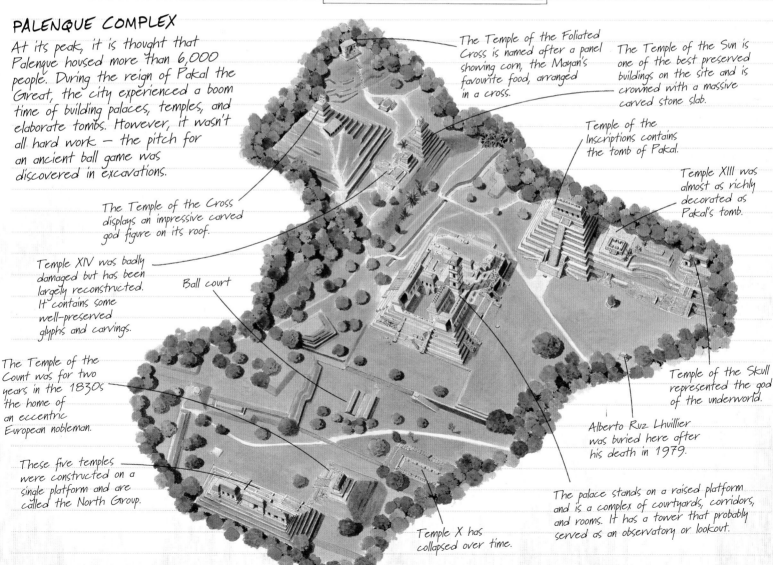

The Temple of the Foliated Cross is named after a panel showing corn, the Mayan's favourite food, arranged in a cross.

The Temple of the Sun is one of the best preserved buildings on the site and is crowned with a massive carved stone slab.

Temple of the Inscriptions contains the tomb of Pakal.

Temple XIII was almost as richly decorated as Pakal's tomb.

The Temple of the Cross displays an impressive carved god figure on its roof.

Temple XIV was badly damaged but has been largely reconstructed. It contains some well-preserved glyphs and carvings.

Ball court

The Temple of the Count was for two years in the 1830s the home of an eccentric European nobleman.

These five temples were constructed on a single platform and are called the North Group.

Temple of the Skull represented the god of the underworld.

Alberto Ruz Lhuillier was buried here after his death in 1979.

Temple X has collapsed over time.

The palace stands on a raised platform and is a complex of courtyards, corridors, and rooms. It has a tower that probably served as an observatory or lookout.

Inside the Temple of the Inscriptions

1 Intricate latticework crowns the top of the temple building.

2 The walls of the temple are decorated with artworks of Mayan gods, which were always shown with blue skin.

3 Carved panels of glyphs tell of Pakal the Great's prosperous 68-year reign over Palenque.

4 The entrance to a stairway that leads down 24 m (80 ft) to the burial chamber.

5 Six priests stand around the tomb and the head priest communicates with the decomposed body of the dead king, sprinking the bones with cinnabar, a red mercury ore.

6 Ventilation ducts lead to air holes on the side of the pyramid.

7 Priests wearing headdresses of green quetzal-bird feathers prepare to sacrifice a jaguar on a stone altar.

8 Warriors, nobles, merchants, wealthy farmers, and their wives and servants crowd at the base of the pyramid to watch the festival.

9 The pyramid has nine steep steps to represent the nine realms of the underworld.

10 The temple was coated with stucco (plaster) containing a pigment to make it bright red.

Temple of Amun, Karnak

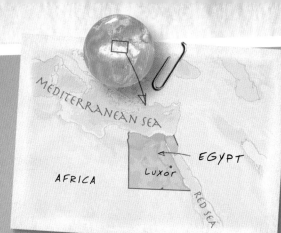

Dear Steve,
Hungry for more? I've got another ancient world to feast your eyes on. It's a religious spot along the River Nile — and it sounds a bit like Amen. But now, a riddle. Too tough, you say? I'll be the judge of that!

A stony jury in this great court. They line the hall — some tall, some short.

How are you finding those figures?

Jack

Stephen Biesty
Dorm 603,
Pakal's Backpacking
Lodge,
Palenque,
Mexico

Construction began at the Karnak complex in ancient Thebes (modern-day Luxor) in the 1500s BCE. The Ancient Egyptian site grew over hundreds of years as the pharaohs (kings) added temples and shrines to worship their gods. Surrounded by vast walls, Karnak's three major temples are dedicated to Mut, Montu, and Amun.

ANCIENT AGRICULTURE

The Ancient Egyptians relied on the fertile banks of the River Nile to grow crops. Every year, the river flooded the land, providing vital water and nutrients for the soil. The Egyptians took food offerings to the temples and asked the gods for good harvests.

"Too tough?" Jack almost made it too easy this time. I'm a big fan of Egyptology, and instantly knew he meant the Temple of Amun. What other spot along the River Nile sounds like amen?

"An ancient world to feast my eyes on." He's right — I can't believe all the sights here.

But there's usually more to Jack's postcards than meets the eye. Maybe "feast" is a clue?

AMUN'S STATUE

The Temple of Amun was built to worship the god Amun. Over centuries, Amun's divine status soared in Ancient Egyptian religion. Originally Amun was the god of wind, then he became god of fertility, before being associated with the sun god, Ra, and becoming the king of the gods. Around the temple, the sphinxes are adorned with rams' heads – Amun's sacred animal.

TEMPLE OF AMUN

Sprawling across 250,000 sq m (2,691,000 sq ft), the Temple of Amun is the largest temple precinct in the Karnak complex. The temple is dedicated to the god Amun and thrived as a place of worship for Ancient Egyptians for 1,300 years. Today, though much of the temple precinct lies in ruins, some areas have been excavated, including the Avenue of Sphinxes (above) that leads to the entrance.

tre

ple
in

EGYPT: Karnak, Temple

GOLDEN BARQUE

Covered in gold and highly decorated, ceremonial boats known as barques were used to transport statues of gods in pilgrimages and festivals.

Temple priests carry a religious statue on a barque.

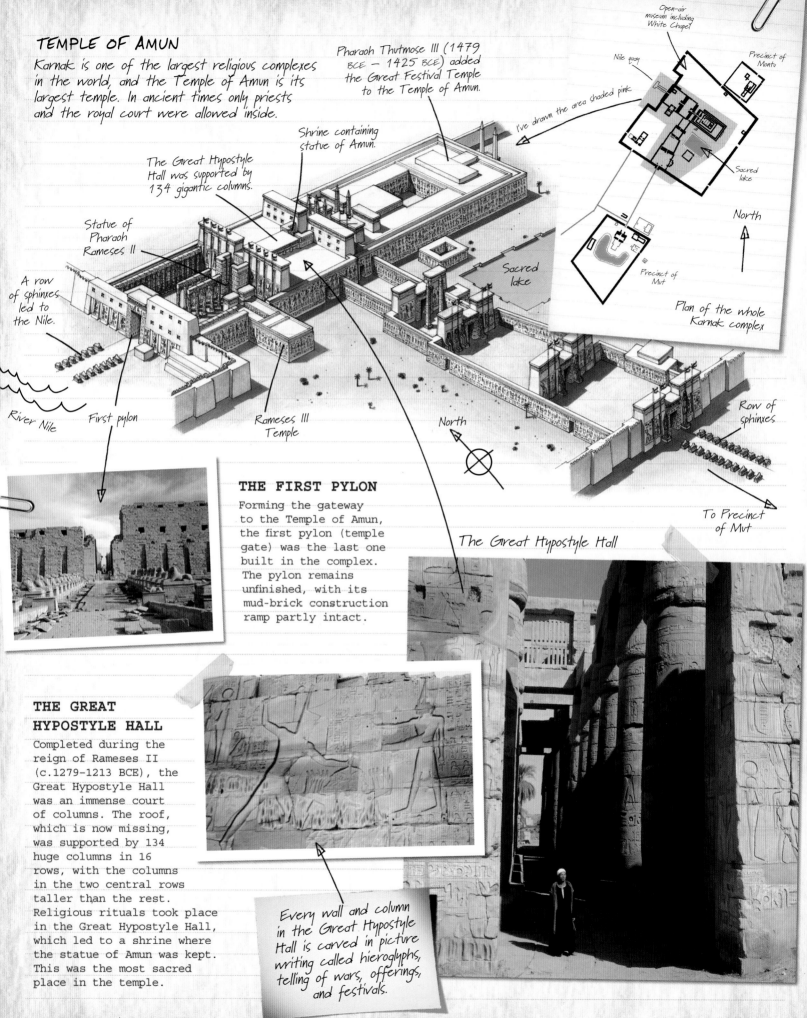

TEMPLE OF AMUN

Karnak is one of the largest religious complexes in the world, and the Temple of Amun is its largest temple. In ancient times only priests and the royal court were allowed inside.

Pharaoh Thutmose III (1479 BCE – 1425 BCE) added the Great Festival Temple to the Temple of Amun.

Shrine containing statue of Amun.

The Great Hypostyle Hall was supported by 134 gigantic columns.

Statue of Pharaoh Rameses II

A row of sphinxes led to the Nile.

River Nile

First pylon

Rameses III Temple

Sacred lake

North

Row of sphinxes

To Precinct of Mut

Open-air museum including White Chapel

Nile quay

Precinct of Montu

I've drawn the area shaded pink

Sacred lake

North

Precinct of Mut

Plan of the whole Karnak complex

THE FIRST PYLON

Forming the gateway to the Temple of Amun, the first pylon (temple gate) was the last one built in the complex. The pylon remains unfinished, with its mud-brick construction ramp partly intact.

The Great Hypostyle Hall

THE GREAT HYPOSTYLE HALL

Completed during the reign of Rameses II (c.1279-1213 BCE), the Great Hypostyle Hall was an immense court of columns. The roof, which is now missing, was supported by 134 huge columns in 16 rows, with the columns in the two central rows taller than the rest. Religious rituals took place in the Great Hypostyle Hall, which led to a shrine where the statue of Amun was kept. This was the most sacred place in the temple.

Every wall and column in the Great Hypostyle Hall is carved in picture writing called hieroglyphs, telling of wars, offerings, and festivals.

But what about the riddle? "A stone jury in this great court." Did they have law courts in Amun? Or is it another sort of court?

"They line the hall – some tall, some short." There is of course the Great Hypostyle Hall – a court filled with stone pillars.

It sounds like the Ancient Egyptians had plenty of feasts but the Beautiful Feast of the Valley was Amun's most important festival. I can't wait to draw the procession making its way through the temple.

Statue of Amun

Every day, priests bathed, dressed, and fed the shrine's statue of Amun as though it were a living person. Did they take him to the loo, too?

TIMELINE

c.1850 BCE
Pharaohs enlarge and beautify the small shrine at Karnak.

c.1530 BCE
Massive building programme begins.

c.1250 BCE
Rameses II builds the Hypostyle Hall. It is so huge that Paris's Notre Dame Cathedral could fit inside it.

c.1069 BCE
The high priests of Amun split Egypt in two, the north (capital in Tanis) ruled by the pharaohs, and the south (capital in Thebes) ruled by the priests of Amun.

663 BCE
The Syrians raid Thebes, carrying off many treasures.

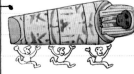

30 BCE
The Romans conquer Egypt. Grain is taken as taxes, and shipped to Rome.

394 CE
The temples fall into ruins and are buried by sand.

1850s
Excavation work on the temple complex begins.

Today
Millions of tourists visit every year.

FESTIVAL FEVER

There were many annual festivals, but the Beautiful Feast of the Valley was one of the most important. The statue of Amun left the temple, carried on an ornate ceremonial barque in a grand procession. It was taken by boat to the west bank of the Nile to visit temples and monuments dedicated to dead pharaohs.

WHITE CHAPEL

Built of alabaster (a milk-white stone) and covered in fine carvings, the White Chapel is the oldest structure within the temple complex. Archaeologists believe it was once coated in gold foil. The statue of Amun was carried to this chapel during processions.

Queen Hatshepsut

I wonder if Hatshepsut means "nice hat" in Egyptian?

QUEEN HATSHEPSUT'S OBELISK

Hatshepsut, one of the few females to become pharaoh, built a towering red granite obelisk in the temple complex. After her reign ended in 1458 BCE, successive rulers purposely blocked the view of the obelisk – and evidence of her once mighty power – by building tall walls around it.

Inside the Temple of Amun

1. The Great Hypostyle Hall is filled with 134 huge columns. During the Beautiful Feast of the Valley, the statue of Amun is carried from its shrine, through the hall, down to the Nile quay.

2. Priests carry the statue of Amun on a ceremonial golden barge. The heavy vessel is supported on poles.

3. Pharaoh Rameses II presides over the procession.

4. Priests spread incense (aromatic spices) before the barque. Some of the priests are dressed in leopard skins.

5. An Avenue of Sphinxes (ram-headed symbols of Amun) leads into the temple.

6. A golden boat waits in the harbour to receive the statue.

7. The statue will sail along the River Nile to the west bank. It is then carried to the royal burial temples there.

8. The towering columns of reddish-brown sandstone are covered in hieroglyphic inscriptions telling of religious festivals and the pharaohs' military triumphs.

9. Stone latticework windows between the pillars flood the court with light.

10. Vast walls surround the temples forming an impenetrable compound. Only priests and royalty are allowed inside.

A final clue

1.30

STEPHEN BIESTY,
c/o KING TUT'S HUTS,
LUXOR,
EGYPT

When I saw CONGRATULATIONS written on the postcard, I thought I had finally reached the end of the quest. Trust Jack to have one more trick up his sleeve.

I am looking at the last two numbers left on my card and Jack's right — I am feeling cross. Where could the key possibly be?

"Where figures meet". Hmmn... perhaps these numbers really do meet! If X marks the spot, the numbers on my card could be my key.

Jack certainly has mapped out this quest very carefully. In the very beginning, he gave me a map. I think I am starting to see how these numbers fit in...

3.45 Saturday,
Flight DK 331
Terminal 1

What a journey!
I can hardly believe
I am so close to
the end...

TRAVEL TICKETS

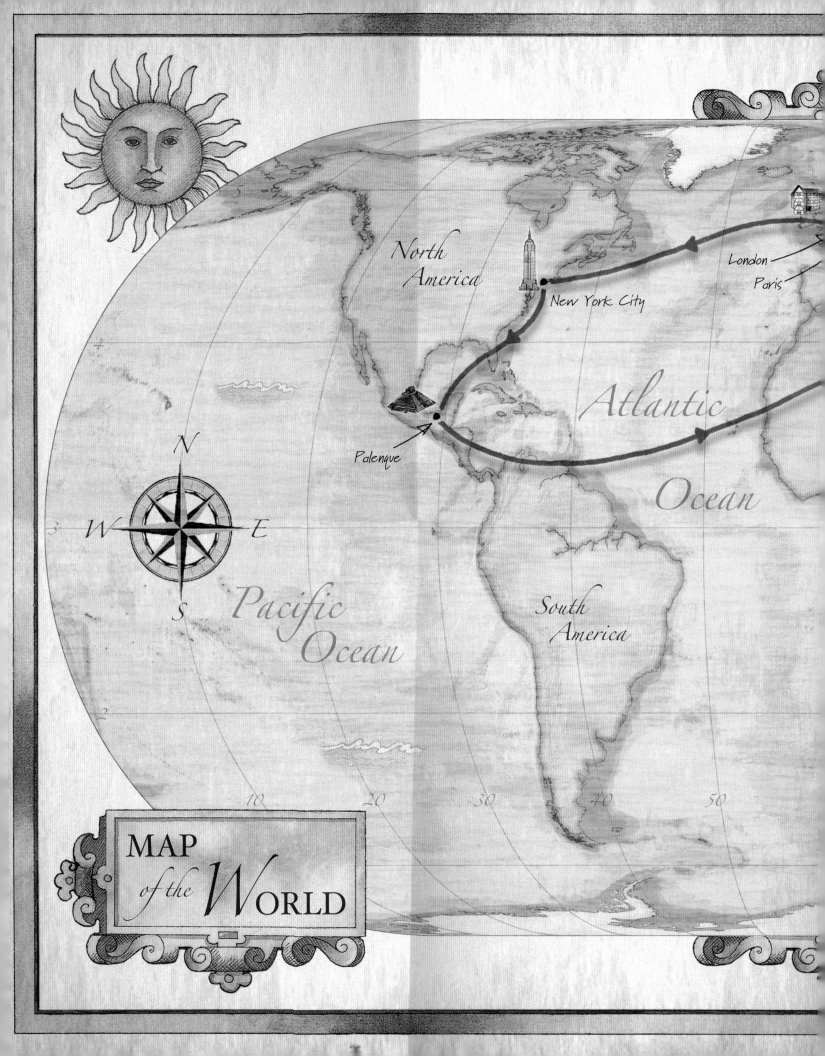

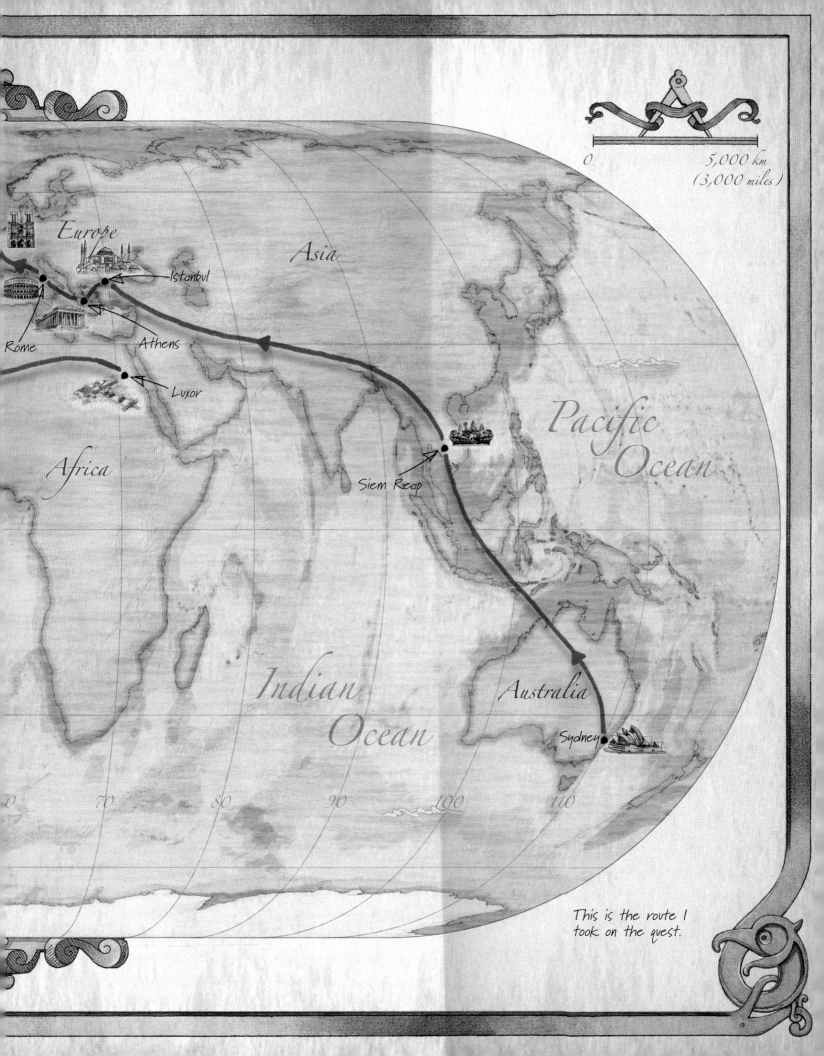

Europe

Asia

Istanbul

Rome

Athens

Luxor

Africa

Siem Reap

Pacific
Ocean

Indian
Ocean

Australia

Sydney

70   80   90   100   110

This is the route I
took on the quest.

0   5,000 km
          (3,000 miles)

To see for yourself
what I discovered, look
in the pocket at the
back of the journal...

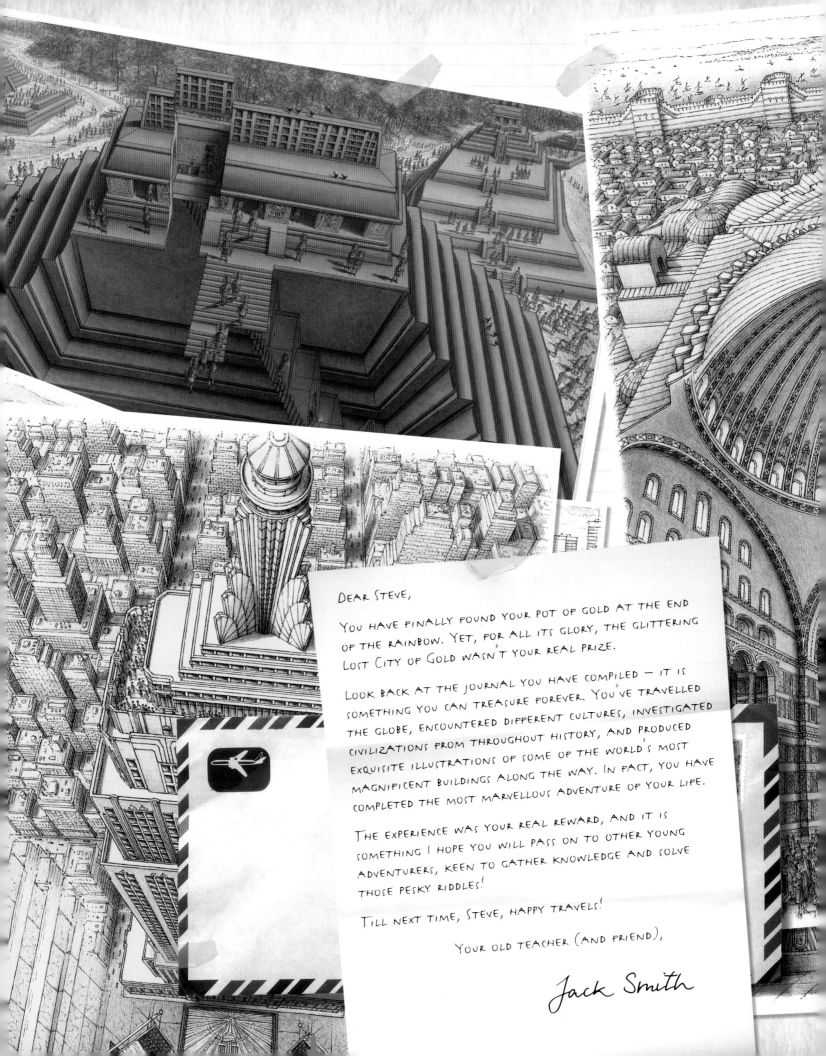

Dear Steve,

You have finally found your pot of gold at the end of the rainbow. Yet, for all its glory, the glittering Lost City of Gold wasn't your real prize.

Look back at the journal you have compiled — it is something you can treasure forever. You've travelled the globe, encountered different cultures, investigated civilizations from throughout history, and produced exquisite illustrations of some of the world's most magnificent buildings along the way. In fact, you have completed the most marvellous adventure of your life.

The experience was your real reward, and it is something I hope you will pass on to other young adventurers, keen to gather knowledge and solve those pesky riddles!

Till next time, Steve, happy travels!

Your old teacher (and friend),

Jack Smith

Super structures

c.3200 BCE
Stonehenge
Bronze-Age stone circle in Wiltshire, England. No one knows for sure exactly what it was built for.

c.1600 BCE
Temple of Amun
Vast temple complex near Luxor, Egypt.

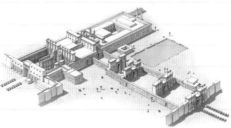

c.228 BCE
Great Wall of China
The longest artificial structure on Earth, stretching 3,500 km (2,150 miles) across China.

c.2560 BCE
Great Pyramid of Giza
A huge pyramid in Egypt, built as a tomb for Pharaoh Khufu.

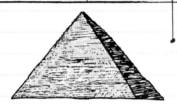

432 BCE
Parthenon
Classical Greek temple in Athens dedicated to Athena, the city's patron goddess.

1420
Forbidden City
Home to the Chinese emperor until 1912, the Forbidden City complex in Beijing consists of 800 buildings with 8,886 rooms.

1346
Himeji Castle
A maze of paths lead up to this Japanese castle to confuse any invaders.

1163
Notre Dame Cathedral
One of the world's most famous gothic cathedrals, Notre Dame has many gruesome-looking gargoyles.

1354
Alhambra
This palace and fortress in Granada, Spain, was the residence of the Muslim kings of southern Spain.

1173
Leaning Tower of Pisa
The bell tower of the cathedral in the Italian city of Pisa leans at an angle because it was built on poorly laid foundations.

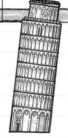

1440
Machu Picchu
Now in ruins, this city was built at the height of the Incan Empire on a mountain ridge in modern-day Peru.

1599
Globe Theatre
Most of Shakespeare's plays were first performed at the Globe in London, England.

1682
Chateau de Versailles
The sprawling palace near Paris, France, was home to the French royal family until the revolution of 1789.

1495
Moscow Kremlin
This fortified complex at the heart of Moscow, Russia, contains four palaces and four cathedrals.

1650
Taj Mahal
Mughal emperor Shah Jahan commissioned the building of the Taj Mahal in Agra, India, as a mausoleum for his wife.

72 CE
Colosseum
The largest amphitheatre of the Roman Empire, used for gladiator fights.

128
Pantheon
Originally an Ancient Roman temple, now a Christian church, this building has the world's largest unreinforced concrete dome.

c.100 BCE
Petra
Many of the buildings in this ancient city are carved into the pink sandstone rock of the desert.

537
Hagia Sophia
Now a state museum, Hagia Sophia was first a Christian church and later converted into a mosque.

683
Temple of the Inscriptions
Pyramid temple built as a tomb for Mayan king Pakal the Great.

c.1000s
Krak des Chevaliers
Christian knights ("crusaders") captured this medieval castle in Syria, fortified it, and made it their headquarters.

1098
Tower of London
This Norman fortress was built by William the Conqueror. It was used as a prison and place of execution for nobles, and today houses the British crown jewels.

1150
Angkor Wat
This stone temple is one of the largest religious complexes in the world.

c.1000s
Great Zimbabwe
An ancient African stone city, once the capital of a great empire.

1889
Eiffel Tower
Named after its designer, Gustave Eiffel, this iron tower in Paris, France, is the most visited monument in the world.

1931
Empire State Building
The 102-storey Art Deco skyscraper is the tallest building in New York City, USA.

2004
Taipei 101
This 509-m- (1,671-ft-) high skyscraper in Taipei, Taiwan, is the tallest building in the world.

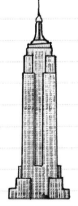

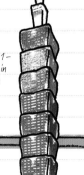

1886
Statue of Liberty
This colossal statue was given to the United States by France. It stands at the mouth of the Hudson River in New York City.

1973
Sydney Opera House
The arts complex in Sydney Harbour is one of the most famous landmarks in Australia.

Glossary

AMBO
A tall platform in a church from where Bible scriptures are read.

AMPHITHEATRE
A public building in Ancient Rome used for spectator sports and games.

ARCHAEOLOGIST
A person who digs up and researches ancient artefacts, historic remains, and buildings.

ARCHITECT
A person who designs and supervises the construction of buildings.

ARENA
The central, sand-covered area of an Ancient Roman amphitheatre.

ART DECO
A popular design style of the 1920s and 1930s featuring geometric shapes.

CATHEDRAL
An important church that is the official seat of a bishop.

CAUSEWAY
A path over a ditch or moat.

CHANCEL
The area around the altar in a church.

COLONNADE
A row of evenly spaced columns.

CRYPT
An underground chamber.

EGYPTOLOGY
A branch of archaeology that specializes in Ancient Egypt.

FLANK
Side of a building.

FRESCO
A painting done on plaster before it dries on a wall.

FRIEZE
A sculptured or decorated horizontal band on a wall.

GALLERY
A raised corridor along a wall.

GARGOYLE
A rain spout for draining a church roof. Gargoyles are usually carved into grotesque figures.

GLYPH
A picture or symbol that conveys information.

HIEROGLYPHS
Ancient Egyptian writing that used pictures and symbols.

LIGHTNING ROD
A metal rod placed on the top of a tall building to protect it from lightning strikes by conducting the electricity from the lightning safely to the ground.

MAUSOLEUM
A large tomb.

MINARET
A tower attached to a mosque. From a balcony on the minaret, an official called a muezzin calls people to prayer.

MOAT
A deep trench surrounding a building, usually filled with water. Moats were designed to deter invaders.

MOSAIC
Art created using small pieces of different coloured stone or glass.

MOSQUE
A Muslim place of worship.

NAVE
The main area of a church.

OBELISK
A tall, thin, four-sided Ancient Egyptian monument topped with a pyramid shape.

PEDIMENT
Decorative, triangular end of a roof crowning the front of a building.

PENDENTIVE
Curved triangular surface that links a dome to the square base beneath.

PORTAL
A grand and impressive entrance.

SANCTUARY
Where sacred objects are kept.

SHRINE
A sacred place of worship often dedicated to a god or religious figure.

SPIRE
A tall structure that tapers to a point. Often found on top of churches.

STOREY
A floor or level of a building.

TEMPLE
A building for religious worship.

VAULT
An arched ceiling or roof.

Index

A

acoustic rings 13
Acropolis, Athens 26, 28-29,
    30-31
actors, Elizabethan 45, 46, 47
airships 51
Alhambra, Spain 76
ambo 24-25, 78
amphitheatre 32-37, 77, 78
Amun *see* Temple of Amun
Angkor Wat, Cambodia 14-19, 77
Art Deco 54-55, 78
Atatürk, Mustafa Kemal 23
Athena 26, 27, 28, 29, 30-31
Athens, Greece 26-31, 77

B

barques 63, 65, 66-67
Bennelong Point, Sydney 9, 11
Big Ben, London 53
Black Death 39
blimps 51
Blue Mosque, Istanbul 23
Brahmins 18-19
Buddhism and Buddhas 15, 16, 17
Burbage, Richard 46
buttresses, flying 39, 41, 42-43
Byzantine crosses 21
Byzantine Empire 20, 21, 22, 29

C

cathedrals 29, 39, 78
Notre Dame de Paris 38-43, 76
Chrysler Building, New York City
    51, 53
churches *see* cathedrals; Hagia
    Sophia
Colosseum, Rome 32-37, 77
columns:
    colonnade 78
    Corinthian 34
    Doric 27, 28, 30-31, 34
    Ionic 27, 28, 34
conic sections 21
Constantine, Roman emperor 23
Constantinople *see* Istanbul

D

Depression, Great 50, 51, 55
dome, floating 22

E

earthquakes 23, 35
Egypt, Ancient 53, 62-67, 76, 78
Eiffel Tower, Paris 39, 53, 77
Elgin marbles 29
Elizabeth I, Queen of England 45
ellipse 21
Empire State Building, New York
    City 50-55, 77

F

festivals 29, 65, 66-67
fire 46, 47, 48-49
Forbidden City, Beijing 76
French Revolution 40, 41
frieze 29, 78

G

gargoyles 39, 42-43, 78
gladiators 34, 35, 36-37
Globe Theatre, London 44-49, 76
glossary 78
glyphs 57, 78
Gothic architecture 39
Great Wall of China 76-77
Great Zimbabwe, Africa 77
Greece, Ancient 26-31, 77
grotesques 39

H

Hagia Sophia, Istanbul 20-25, 77
Hatshepsut, Queen of Egypt 65
Hekatombion 29
hieroglyphs 57, 64, 78
Himeji Castle, Japan 76
Hinduism 15, 17, 19
Hunchback of Notre Dame 39, 41
Hypostyle Hall, Great 64, 65,
    66-67

I

Isidore of Miletus 21
Istanbul (formerly
    Constantinople) 20-25

J

Justinian I, Roman Emperor 21,
    23, 24-25

K

Karnak *see* Temple of Amun
Khmer Empire 14, 15, 17
Krak des Chevaliers, Syria 77
Kremlin, Moscow 76

L

Leaning Tower of Pisa, Italy 76
London, UK 44-49, 53, 76, 77
Luxor, Egypt 62-67

M

Machu Picchu, Peru 76
Mayan civilization 56-61
minarets 22, 78
mosaics 22, 23, 78
mosques 20, 22, 23, 29, 78
mythology:
    Greek 26, 27, 28
    Mayan 59, 61

N

Napoleon Bonaparte 41
New York City, USA 50-55
Nile, River, Egypt 63, 65, 66-67
Notre Dame Cathedral, Paris
    38-43, 76

O

obelisk 65, 78
Organ, Grand 11, 13
Ottomans 20, 22, 23, 29

P

Pakal the Great, Mayan King 57,
    58-59, 60-61
Palenque, Mexico 56-61
Paris, France 38-43, 53, 77
Parthenon, Athens 26-31, 77
pendentives 22, 24-25, 78
pediment 28, 78
Petra, Jordan 77
Plato 27
popes 35, 38
Puritans 45, 47
pyramids: Great Pyramid of Giza
    53, 76
    Temple of the Inscriptions,
    Palenque 56-61, 77

R

Rameses II, Pharoah of Egypt 64,
    65, 66-67
Rome, Ancient 21, 32-37, 65,
    77, 78
rose window 40, 41, 42-43
Roskob, John J. 51, 53
Ruz Lhuillier, Alberto 57, 59

S

Shakespeare, William 44, 45, 46,
    47, 48-49
skyscrapers 51, 52, 53
Statue of Liberty, New York City
    77
Stonehenge, England 76
Suryavarman II, Khmer King 14,
    15, 19
Sydney Opera House, Australia
    8-13, 77

T

Taj Mahal, India 76
Tapei 101 tower, Taiwan 77
Temple of Amun, Karnak 62-67, 76
Temple of the Inscriptions,
    Palenque 56-61, 77
Thebes, Ancient *see* Luxor
Tower of London, England 77
Trajan, Roman emperor 35, 37
trireme 29

U

Utzon, Jørn 9, 11

V

vault 42-43, 78
Versailles, France 76-77
Vespasian, Roman Emperor 33, 35
Vishnu 15, 19
vomitoria 34, 36-37

W

World Trade Center, New York City
    53

Acknowledgements

Dorling Kindersley would like to thank: Professor Sir John Boardman, Dr Brian O'Callaghan, Dr Anne Millard, David Murdoch, Philip Parker, and Dr Peter Sharrock for advising on the main artworks; Alice Buller, Dan Hooke, and Theo Hooke for testing the riddles; and Jackie Brind for the index.

Picture credits

Artworks on pages 12–13, 18–19, 24–25, 30–31, 36–37, 42–43, 48–49, 54–55, 60–61, 66–67, and poster by Stephen Biesty. Other artworks by Stefan Podhorodecki, and Laszlo Veres of Beehive Illustration.

The publisher would like to thank the following for their kind permission to reproduce their photographs:

(Key: a-above; b-below/bottom; c-centre; f-far; l-left; r-right; t-top)
Alamy Images: David Ball 11tr; **Archivo Celia Gutierrez vda. de Ruz**: 57tr; **The Art Archive**: Galleria Estense, Modena / Dagli Orti (A) 35tr; National Anthropological Museum Mexico / Dagli Orti 57cl, 58br; Dagli Orti 22t; **The Bridgeman Art Library**: Dulwich Picture Gallery, London, UK 46cl; Giraudon 35fcl; Karnak Temple, Karnak, Egypt, Giraudon 65tr; Museo Nacional de Antropologia, Mexico City, Mexico/Boltin Picture Library 56crb, 58c; Phoenix Art Museum, Arizona, USA 34tl; San Vitale, Ravenna, Italy, Giraudon 21t; Woburn Abbey, Bedfordshire, UK 45tr; **The Trustees of the British Museum**: 28br; **Corbis**: Yann Arthus-Bertrand 20t; David Ball 50–51; Bettmann 51br, 53cl; Gillian Darley; Edifice 46tl; Leonard de Selva 41tl; Sebastien Desarmaux/Godong 15t; Philip Gendreau/Bettmann 51cla; Joson/zefa 14–15; Christophe Loviny 14crb; Kevin R. Morris 16bc, 16crb, 17tr; Bill Ross 38; Luca I. Tettoni 17tl; Sandro Vannini 65cl; Adam Woolfitt 23t; **De Agostini Editore**: DEA PICTURE LIBRARY 21cr; **DK Images**: Archaeological Receipts Fund (TAP) 26crb; Ashmolean Museum, Oxford 39br; British Museum 27cb, 28cr, 29tr, 63t, 65bc; CONACULTA-INAH-MEX. Authorized reproduction by the Instituto Nacional de Antropologia e Historia. 57cra, 58tr; Rough Guides 27br, 34bl, 40bl, 40br, 40t; Sydney Opera House Trust 10ca, 10cla, 10tl; Vatican Museums and Galleries, Rome 33ca; **Getty Images**: Kenneth Garrett 56; Louis Grandadam/Stone 58tl; Peter Hendrie/The Image Bank 8; Hulton Archive/Keystone 9bl; Andrea Pistolesi 47t; **The Kobal Collection**: RKO 53cr; **Nashville Convention & Visitors Bureau**: Gary Layda 28bl; **NSW Lotteries**: 9t; **PA Photos**: Rob Griffith/AP 11tl; **Pentagram**: based on shop drawings by McCurdy & Co.: 46cra; **Rex Features**: SNAP 41tr; **Merle Greene Robertson**: 59tc; **Shakespeare's Globe**: Nik Milner 44c; **South American Pictures**: 59tl; **Sydney Opera House**: Courtesy Sydney Opera House Trust 10tr, 11cl; **Wikipedia, The Free Encyclopedia**: 33br, 45cl; David Corby 53br; Charles J Sharp 15crb.

Sticker sheet picture credits
The Bridgeman Art Library: cra (sheet 1: mask); crb (sheet 1: mosaic); **DK Images**: British Museum br (sheet 1: horse's head), fcrb (sheet 1: statue head).

All other images © Dorling Kindersley

For further information see: www.dkimages.com

ANSWERS TO THE RIDDLES: p.8, 10, 154, p.14, 1,000, p.20, 40, p.26, 17, p.32, 4, p.38, 28, p.44, 8, p.50, 73, p.56, 617, p.62, 134